The Church Music
of
William Billings

Da Capo Press Music Reprint Series

GENERAL EDITOR

FREDERICK FREEDMAN

VASSAR COLLEGE

J. MURRAY BARBOUR

The Church Music
of
William Billings

DA CAPO PRESS • NEW YORK • 1972

Library of Congress Cataloging in Publication Data

Barbour, James Murray, 1897-
   The church music of William Billings.

   (Da Capo Press music reprint series)
   Reprint of the 1960 ed.
   Bibliography: p.
   1. Billings, William, 1746-1800. Works, vocal.
I. Title.
[ML410.B588B4   1972]   783′.026   72-39000
ISBN 0-306-70434-X

This Da Capo Press edition of
The Church Music of William Billings
is an unabridged republication of the first edition
published in East Lansing, Michigan, in 1960. It is
reprinted by special arrangement with Michigan State
University Press.

Copyright 1960 Michigan State University Press

Published by Da Capo Press, Inc.
A Subsidiary of Plenum Publishing Corporation
227 West 17th Street
New York, New York 10011

The Church Music of William Billings

The Church Music

of

William Billings

J. MURRAY BARBOUR

MICHIGAN STATE UNIVERSITY PRESS

TO MARY
Who erroneously calls herself "General Public"

Contents

Preface   ix

Introduction   xi

Texts   1

Rhythm and Meter   14

Melody   43

Counterpoint and Harmony   66

Modality and Tonality   100

Texture and Form. Conclusion   119

Appendix A: Alphabetical Index of Billings' Psalm Tunes   139

Appendix B: Index of Billings' Anthems by Texts   147

Appendix C: Selective Index of Billings' Psalm Tunes by Texts   151

Appendix D: Index of Non-Billings' Psalm Tunes   154

Appendix E: Index of Non-Billings' Anthems by Texts   156

Appendix F: Source of Secular Examples   158

Bibliography   159

Index   165

Preface

The genesis of my book on Billings' church music is as haphazard as these things usually are. A dozen years ago a seminar report on one of George Pullen Jackson's books led to a Collegium Musicum program of early American church music which included Billings' *David's Lamentation*. Later I examined a number of Billings' anthems with the view of presenting an entire Billings program. Although this never materialized, I extended my study to all of Billings' anthems, and presented the results as a paper before the Midwest Chapter of the American Musicological Society in Iowa City on April 18, 1953.

The following year, in Vienna, I gave three lectures on Billings and American church music. After my return home I read Ralph T. Daniel's excellent dissertation on the New England anthem, and then rewrote my anthem paper as an article. But it grew into a monster—fifty pages in length, plus one hundred and nine musical examples! Paul Henry Lang, erudite scholar, editor, and critic, sagely recommended in the summer of 1956 that I expand the article into a book. Irving Lowens, indefatigable delver into early American psalm tunes and psalmodists, warmly supported Lang's idea.

Thanks to a grant from Michigan State University, photostats and microfilm prints of psalm tunes by Billings and certain of his English and American contemporaries were obtained from the Library of Congress in Washington and the William L. Clements Library in Ann Arbor. It has been a pleasure to do research in both of these libraries, for the completeness of their coverage in this field is equalled by the courteous helpfulness of the attendants.

After this new material had been digested, I set down various characteristics of the psalm tunes, and then meshed this account into what had previously been written about the anthems. I hope

Preface

the seams do not show overmuch! Most of the final writing was done in an old farmhouse on the slope of the Tuscarora Mountain in southern Pennsylvania.

William Dinneen, who in 1950 had prepared a study of Billings' music for the use of his students at Brown University, graciously allowed me to borrow this material for the greater part of a year. It has been invaluable in the preparation of some of the bibliographical lists given at the end of the book. I wish to thank Mr. Dinneen for personal assistance on recondite points which have kept cropping up. I should like to convey my thanks also to Ralph Daniel in Bloomington and to Irving Lowens in Washington; they have unselfishly shared with me some of their substantial knowledge of Billings and his contemporaries.

"The Texts of Billings' Church Music" appeared in *Criticism*, Vol. 1, No. 1, Winter 1959. This is a publication of Wayne State University.

The profuse musical examples, which add so greatly to the value of my book, have also added greatly to the cost of publishing it. The Michigan State University Research Fund has relieved the Michigan State University Press of part of this burden by a generous grant, for which the Press and I are very grateful.

J. Murray Barbour
East Lansing, Michigan
April, 1960

Introduction

Both in the extent and the substance of his work, William Billings was the most important composer of the pioneer period of American church music, the last third of the 18th century. His compositions consisted of anthems and psalm tunes—sacred music except for a handful of the anthems. In his own day Billings was much admired. But even before his death a change of taste in church music had begun to take place, and this became so pronounced in a few years that Billings was almost completely forgotten except in certain rural sections of the South.

In recent years an antiquarian interest in Americana has resulted in the publishing of some of Billings' psalms and anthems, including examples of the "fuguing tunes" with which he is chiefly, but erroneously, associated in the popular mind. Those who have sampled the music have found it fresh and enjoyable. They fail to understand why so many writers on musical subjects during the past half century have been both derogatory and patronizing in their appraisal of Billings' work. These detractors agree that he had tremendous enthusiasm and a certain dramatic flair; but, once these admissions have been made, the barbs have been thrust in deeply. Thus Louis C. Elson[1] described Billings as "a great music-lover, and enthusiast, honest in his convictions, but uncouth in expression and utterly untrained in the school of music which he undertook to compose." John Tasker Howard,[2] after quoting Billings' panegyric of the fuguing tune (See p. 67), comments, "Such an imagination, and such enthu-

[1] From *The National Music of America and Its Sources*, by Louis C. Elson, copyright 1924 by L. C. Page and Co., Inc. Used by permission of L. C. Page Co., Inc., a subsidiary of Farrar, Straus and Cudahy, Inc.

[2] John Tasker Howard, *Our American Music*, Revised Ed., New York: Thomas Y. Crowell Co., 1939, p. 46.

Introduction

siasm should surely have produced masterpieces, but, alas, no—merely the crude attempts of a tanner to produce something different, a striving for effects he could imagine, but for which he lacked the necessary equipment." Carl E. Lindstrom[3] has called Billings "a virtually illiterate composer," and has quoted approvingly from a manuscript work by Nathan H. Allen, "Musically worthless, these books command attention only as ancient milestones from which we have learned the way to higher and better things as we left them behind." Hamilton C. Macdougall[4] also speaks of "an entire absence of all harmonic culture" in Billings, as well as "musical illiteracy" in the New England composers *en masse*. Of course, most of these benevolent critics like also to emphasize Billings' admitted physical peculiarities (blind eye, withered arm, game leg, harsh voice, and habit of taking snuff), so that in the end one is left with the impression that he was a cross between a yahoo and a dancing bear!

The main events of Billings' life are well known. He was born in Boston in 1746, had a common-school education, was apprenticed to a tanner and continued to practice that trade for the rest of his life. His knowledge of music was obtained largely, if not wholly, from reading and observation, although he is said to have studied with John Barry, a local singer and choir leader. His musical activities consisted of organizing and conducting singing schools in various towns in the Boston area. Despite the great popularity of his compositions, he was in straitened circumstances for the last decade of his life and died in real poverty in 1800, leaving a widow and six children.

In 1770, at the age of 24, Billings published his first collection of hymns and anthems, *The New England Psalm Singer,* to be followed by five others—*The Singing Master's Assistant,* 1778; *Music in Miniature* (hymns only), 1779; *The Psalm Singer's Amusement,* 1781; *The Suffolk Harmony,* 1786, and *The Continental Harmony,* 1794. These contain over 250 different hymn tunes and nearly 50 anthems. *Music in Miniature* has contributed

[3] Carl E. Lindstrom, "William Billings and His Times," *Musical Quarterly,* Vol. 25, 1939, pp. 479-497.

[4] Hamilton C. Macdougall, *Early New England Psalmody,* Brattleboro, Stephen Daye Press, 1940, p. 61f.

so little to the total picture of Billings the composer that it was largely ignored in the present study.

Just how illiterate was Billings? It is the opinion of the present writer that Billings' detractors are almost totally wrong in their criticisms. His works do contain glaring faults and weaknesses; but they are seldom those of which he has been accused. To call him illiterate betrays a lack of familiarity with Billings' music, or else a failure to comprehend what musical illiteracy really is. Even his spelling was good—excellent for his time and place. It has been modernized in this book, where no attempt is made to emphasize Billings' "quaintness." He used correctly eleven Italian terms for tempo and mood: Adagio, Allegro, Affetuoso, Divoto, Grave, Lamentatione, Largo, Maestoso, Presto, Vigoroso, and Vivace. (More of these terms occur in his earlier publications than in the later.) For dynamics he used piano, forte, and fortissimo (Choro Grando was the equivalent of fortissimo), with a crescendo indicated by "swell" or, once, in Percy Grainger fashion, by "shout and swell." His metrical signatures include $\frac{6}{8}$, $\frac{2}{4}$, $\frac{3}{4}$, $\mathcal{C}$, $[\frac{4}{4}]$ $\frac{6}{4}$, $\mathcal{D}$ $[\frac{2}{2}]$ and $\frac{3}{2}$; these were almost always used correctly, especially in his later works. It is true that Billings' first collection, NEPS, contained many errors of notation, the most heinous being the omission of accidentals. But for this the engraver was at least partly to blame: he was Paul Revere, who probably does deserve to be called musically illiterate, however skilled he may have been in equitation.

Billings' literacy should become quickly apparent in the chapters which follow, where the elements of his style are reduced to his choice of texts, his rhythmic freedom, his melodic variety, his contrapuntal practice with its reflections upon harmony and modality, and his musical form. Both Ralph Daniel[5] and Irving Lowens[6] have shown that Billings followed an English tradition. But even so well-informed a writer as Macdougall could ask himself the question, "What influence did the English psalmody have upon his [Billings'] music?" and answer it, "None at

[5] Ralph Thomas Daniel, *The Anthem in New England Before 1800*, Harvard dissertation, Feb., 1955.

[6] Irving Lowens, "The Origins of the American Fuging Tune," *Journal of the American Musicological Society*, Vol. 6, 1953, pp. 43-52.

Introduction

all."[7] To refute Macdougall's wholly fallacious conclusion, adequate attention is paid in this book to the sacred works of Billings' immediate predecessors in England—Tans'ur, Arnold, Knapp, and the rest. To get the proper perspective on Billings as a New England composer, such American contemporaries as Read, Holden, and Shumway have also not been neglected. Thus, in addition to Billings' own volumes, eleven collections of 18th century English and American psalmody were examined for the study of the psalm tunes and almost as many for the study of the anthems; the complete list may be found in the bibliography.

The music examined in the present study was written for four mixed voices—treble, counter, tenor, and bass. The older names for the female voices have been replaced in this book by the modern equivalents—soprano and alto. Except in responsorial or imitative passages, the principal melody was always in the tenor. The notation was in open score. When the music was homophonic, the text would appear once, between the alto and tenor parts. But even in the more polyphonic passages, there would often be only a tag in some of the voices, and when words were repeated to different music the symbol ∺ regularly indicated the repeated text. Very frequently the latter part of a psalm tune would be repeated, the Dal segno symbol (:S:) being used instead of dots.

There was no uniformity in the clefs used by the English composers. Adams used three G clefs and an F clef, both the alto and tenor being written an octave higher than the actual pitch. Adams' practice was followed by Lyon and Williams. Arnold used a G clef, the alto and tenor C clefs, and an F clef—a practice reminiscent of exercises in strict counterpoint. A few of Lyon's tunes are notated like Arnold's. Both Law and Church notated their three-voice tunes (soprano, tenor, bass) with two G clefs and an F clef. For his four-voice tunes Church used two G clefs, a tenor clef, and an F clef. Tans'ur used a G clef, an alto clef, a G clef, and an F clef. His practice was followed by Billings and all the remaining American composers in this study.

In performances of the New England anthems today, the propriety of instrumental accompaniment is a moot question.

[7] Macdougall, *op. cit.*, p. 50.

Introduction

Clarence Dickinson has not hesitated to add organ accompaniments to the Billings' anthems which he has edited. Oliver Daniel, however, in Billings' works published by Birchard, has presented them unaccompanied, although with soprano and tenor parts interchanged. It is quite unnecessary to interchange these parts: if the tenor part is doubled in the higher octave by one or two sopranos, as was the New England custom, the balance is right. These sopranos drop out in the fuguing passages, or else join the other sopranos.

The English anthems, as originally published, had a figured continuo part. (The Moravian anthems in this country were accompanied, and, in those by J. F. Peter particularly, the style is much more instrumental than vocal. They, however, did not have the wide dissemination of the New England anthems.) When these anthems were first published in this country, the figures were usually omitted, although occasionally a sharp might remain, as an indication of a major third. With solo voices, an added continuo might also remain, as in Tans'ur's *Psalm 104*. (Example 31) The English anthems also had organ "symphonies," and these too were usually deleted in New England, a strange remnant appearing in an anthem by Stephenson ("Sing, O ye heavens"), where at the beginning there are eighteen bars of rest for the (unprinted) "sym.," as well as seven, ten, and five bars of rest later. (The clash in Example 155 from Stephenson would be minimized if the half-note F sharp in the alto were played instead of sung; similarly, Gram's dry and clashing bass in Example 132 cries aloud for an instrument.)

The only independent organ parts in Billings' church music are the two short instrumental interludes in the anthem, "O thou to whom," the first of these being called "Sym. to introduce B flat." Since only five Episcopal churches and no Congregational meeting-houses in Boston had organs at Billings' time, the need for an organ part would have been slight. Except for this one anthem, all of Billings' music was printed as unaccompanied vocal music, despite doubts one may have about the rendition of some of the apparent duets between the bass and a higher voice. (See p. 129) This negative evidence does not preclude the use of any accompaniment, since Billings is said to have had the credit of introducing the 'cello as an accompanying instrument.

Introduction

When "choosing" notes in the bass were in octaves (See p. 120), the lower note was often uncomfortably low for a singer and the 'cello would have been a logical choice.

One must be on guard against the excesses of printed accompaniments in modern editions of Billings' works, since, for example, Dickinson has grossly exaggerated the modal character of "Be glad then, America," his worst offense being the added accompaniment to a short bass solo which is unashamedly in E flat major, but which is harmonized as Aeolian mode. But, in my opinion, a discreet organ accompaniment today would offend only the most rabid adherents to what is erroneously considered to be the only true *a cappella* style.

Texts

In the choice of texts for his psalm tunes Billings allied himself with the most progressive church composers of his time. The Old Version of Sternhold and Hopkins was still highly regarded in England in the middle of the 18th century, although in general its phraseology sounds harsh and awkward today. From it Billings chose only one text, "The Lord descended from above," (part of Psalm 18), which he also used in an anthem. Although the New Version of Tate and Brady was far more popular with Billings, fewer than twenty of his psalm texts were drawn from it. The most popular treasury of Billings' texts, by far, was provided by Isaac Watts. Some 65 of the tunes are settings of Watts's psalms and hymns.

The most intriguing thing in the choice of texts by Billings is his setting of eighteen poems by "Relly." The reference is to *Christian Hymns, Poems, and Spiritual Songs . . .* , by James and John Relly, which was first published in 1758. There is no doubt that Billings was familiar with this work, for in the edition of 1776 it is noted in the list of subscribers that Mr. William Billings had purchased two copies.

James Relly, 1722(?)-1778, was an English-born Universalist minister, whose convert, John Murray, was to found the Universalist church in America. Relly published sermons and a number of theological works, in addition to the above-mentioned collection of religious poetry, of which his brother John was coauthor. Apparently Billings was very greatly impressed with the Relly poetry at the time that he was working on the *Suffolk Harmony*, for all eighteen of the Relly texts are to be found there. (Three of the texts and tunes reappear in other Billings collections.) Of the eighteen, fourteen are by James Relly and the other four by John.

The collection of George Whitefield is credited with five texts, of which three were by Charles Wesley and two by John

Cennick. The Rev. Dr. Mather Byles, eminent Congregational minister of Boston, was the author of four texts; the "late" Samuel Byles, M.D. and John Peck each penned two. Addison's metrical version of Psalm 23, "The Lord my pasture shall prepare," is set in the *Continental Harmony*.

Billings himself contributed only two texts, the patriotic *Chester* ("Let tyrants shake their iron rod") and the Christmas hymn, *Shiloh* ("Methinks I see a heav'nly host"). A mystery exists concerning P.M., who is credited with five texts in the *New England Psalm Singer* and another in the *Singing Master's Assistant*. These initials do not stand for Particular Meter, for the meter is also indicated for these psalm tunes; nor do they fit any of the better known psalmists of the 18th century.

An even dozen of Billings' psalm texts are supposed to be anonymous, either by direct statement or for want of other attribution. However, this list includes the New Version "Sing to the Lord a newmade song," Tate's "While shepherds watched," Watts's "Awake, my heart" and "Shepherds, rejoice," together with such genuine instances as the carol, "A virgin unspotted," and the Easter hymn, "Jesus Christ is ris'n today."

So numerous are the tunes in familiar meters in any collection of the 18th century that one may hastily assume that nothing was ever sung that was not in one of the iambic stanza forms: S.M. (Short Meter—6686), C.M. (Common Meter—8686), or L.M. (Long Meter—8888), or else in double, eight-line stanzas of these three meters. The normal rhyme scheme for the above meters is, of course, *abab*. We shall take no especial consideration of the not uncommon *xaxa* stanza, nor of the Long Meter *abba* variant. Internal rhyme also occurs, albeit rarely, as in John Peck's "Here is a song, which doth belong / To all the human race."

Four-fifths of Billings' tunes were in familiar meters. But greater interest lies in some of the more than fifty others that were marked P.M. It is not at all surprising that there should have been many Particular Meters among these texts, since, in the main, these were metrical psalms, as the name "psalm tune" implies, and these had had a bewildering variety of meter ever since the completion of the Old Version in the 16th century. The

Old Version contained forty-three different meters, the most frequent being L. M. Double. Many of the rarer meters followed the more intricate stanza forms of the Genevan and Anglo-Genevan prototypes. Although the New Version ran largely to C.M. and L.M. texts, its Supplement gave new texts that could be sung to a dozen P.M. tunes of the Old Version. Isaac Watts, also, employed some of the less usual meters.

The most popular of the Particular Meters was 66664444, the meter for the Old Version Psalm 148. It occurs eleven times in Billings' collections, and in eight of the other collections examined. It is also the meter of the New Version Psalm 136 and of Watts's Psalm 84. (Frequently it was referred to as the Hallelujah Meter.) In the Old Version Psalm 148 the rhyme scheme is *ababcddc:*

> Give laud unto the Lord
> From heav'n that is so high;
> Praise him in deed and word
> Above the starry sky.
>> And also ye,
>> His angels all,
>> Armies royal,
>> Praise joyfully.

The same scheme is found in the New Version Psalm 148 and in two of Watts's texts. In another of Watts's texts the second quatrain rhymes as in the Old Version-New Version models, but the first quatrain has only one rhyme:

> To spend one sacred day,
> Where God and saints abide,
> Affords diviner joys
> Than thousand days besides.

The Tate and Brady Psalm 136 ("To God, the mighty Lord") has the more regular rhyme scheme, *ababcdcd*. Here is its second quatrain:

> For God does prove
> Our constant friend;
> His boundless love
> Shall never end.

Charles Wesley's familiar, "Rejoice, the Lord is King," has two rhymes in the first quatrain, but only one in the refrain:

> Lift up your heart, lift up your voice;
> Rejoice, again I say, rejoice.

Finally, at the opposite pole from the elegant rhyme scheme of the Old Version Psalm 148, there is a text which has only one rhyme in each quatrain, *xaxaxbxb*. It too should be given complete:

> Not all the pow'rs on earth
> Joined in a league with hell,
> Can disconcert our plan,
> Which nothing can excell.
> > Since such a friend
> > In God we find,
> > Adieu to fears
> > Of ev'ry kind.

Thus Billings has included four interesting variants of the original 66664444 stanza, and his overall use of the Hallelujah Meter represents one of the most vital elements in his psalm tunes.

Another popular Old Version meter is that for Psalm 50 (10 10 10 10 11 11), as set by Billings and others to Watts's text, "The God of glory sends his summons forth." Still another is that for Psalm 85 (886886), which Billings has used twice. The Old Version meter for Psalms 112 and 127, also used several times by Tate and Brady, is 888888, *i.e.*, L.M., six lines. It occurs five times in Billings' works.

Iambic pentameter, so popular in English poetry in the sonnet, blank verse, and the heroic couplet, was the meter for the Old Version Psalm 110 (10 10 10 10), and is much sung in our churches today, as in such contrasted hymns as "Abide with me" and "God of our fathers." Strangely enough, only one example of this meter was found in any of the sixteen collections examined. This was a setting by Billings of a text by James Relly. Since it is unique, it is given herewith:

> All over lovely is my Lord and God,
> When nailed on Calv'ry to a cross of wood.
> My praise attends his blood, his name I'll bless;
> He is my wisdom, strength, and righteousness.

The six-line iambic pentameter stanza (10 10 10 10 10 10) is as ancient as the Ainsworth Psalter, where it is used for Psalm 54, and is also the meter for the New Version Psalm 50. Billings has set it in Watts's text, "Not to our names, Thou only just and true." Watts's setting of Psalm 122 was in the iambic meter, 668668; Billings and others have set this text, "How pleased and blest was I."

Another popular meter was the trochaic 7777, which Billings set twice, his tune *Resurrection* being the familiar Easter hymn, "Jesus Christ is ris'n today," with Hallelujahs. Another rather frequent trochaic meter with Hallelujahs, set by Billings and his contemporaries, is 878787. "Sing the triumphs," a poem by James Relly in this meter, has so many run-on lines that the meter is practically 15 15. See especially stanza two:

> Long he struggled with confusèd
> Noise and garments rolled in blood,
> Till, destroying sin, and hell, and
> Death, he rescued Man to God.

A more complicated meter, 76767876, alternately trochaic and iambic, was also not too rare, and Billings has set two poems by the adventurous James Relly in it.

The Old Version meter for Psalm 104 was taken by Tate and Brady for Psalm 149 (10 10 11 11), "O praise ye the Lord." This is in amphibrachs, with a catatectic second foot in the first two lines. Billings has set this New Version text and also the favorite Wesley hymn, "Ye servants of God." (With internal rhyme throughout, the latter might be listed as 55556565.) Too often the study of metrics stops short of describing the amphibrachic foot, which is much more at home in English poetry than either dactyls or anapests. The nursery rhyme, "Ride a cock horse," for example, is largely in amphibrachs, with a 9 11 11 10 stanza.

Two Christmas carols set by Billings, "A Virgin unspotted" and "As shepherds in Jewry," have the more regular amphibrach meter, 11 11 11 11. Although it would seem as if such a folklike and jiggy meter would not be rare, no further examples have been located in all of the collections examined. One amphibrachic text set by Billings masquerades in his *Singing Master's Assistant* as Long Meter. This is Wesley's "Ah, lovely appearance of death," which indeed has eight syllables in each line, but is in amphibrachic trimeter rather than in iambic tetrameter. Billings' confusion may be excused, for 20th century hymnals are likely to commit such errors as including with the iambic pentameter texts a dactylic tetrameter text like Bonar's "Blessing and honor and glory and pow'r."

Other variants of the amphibrachic tetrameter are James Relly's "What beauties divine" (10 11 10 11) and his brother's "Thou art my best portion" (11 6 6 11 11), with internal rhyme splitting the second line. There is also a six-line stanza by James Relly, "O Love, what a secret to mortals thou art" (11 11 10 11 11 11). All of these poems have, of course, been set by Billings.

Sapphic meter implies Horace's *Integer vitae* to former Latin students, who perhaps have sung it to Flemming's melody. Paradoxically, this tune is found in our hymnals today as a setting for Charlotte Elliott's "O Holy Savior, Friend unseen," which is not in Sapphics at all, but in the iambic meter, 8886! The true Sapphic meter is 11 11 11 5, predominatingly trochaic, but with an initial dactyl in each line. This meter is not uncommon either in modern hymnals, as in Catherine Winkworth's translation of Petrus Herbert's evening hymn, "Now God be with us." But neither this nor other hymns in the real Sapphic meter are ordinarily set to the Flemming tune! Billings has made a fine setting of Sapphics for Watts's ode, *The Day of Judgment,* the first stanza of which is:

> When the fierce Northwind with his airy forces
> Rears up the Baltic to a foaming fury,
> And the red lightning with a storm of hail comes
> Rushing amain down.

After eight stanzas in unrhymed Sapphics, the original ode concludes with fourteen more in Common Meter.

Three of James Relly's unique meters are trochaic: "Glorious Jesus," with 85857785 meter; "All is hush," with 77775777, and "My belovèd, haste away," with 787878, the last two lines being a refrain.

English verse shies away from dactyls, except for substituted initial feet and for self-conscious imitations of classical meters.

Billings has set an anonymous text that is predominantly in dactyls:

> Father of mercies,
> Thou fountain of graces,
>   One God evermore.
> Author of harmony,
> Hater of tyranny,
> Essence of majesty,
>   Thee we adore!

The above stanza (5656664) closely resembles "My country, 'tis of thee," whose meter is 6646664. One probably does not realize how closely our National Hymn, nominally in iambs, approachs dactyls through initial trochees. Take, for example: "Land where my fathers died, Land of the pilgrims' pride," "Land of the noble free," "Author of liberty," and "Long may our land be bright." "God save the Queen" has even more striking examples of dactyls, such as "Send her victorious, Happy and glorious, Long to reign over us," "Scatter her enemies," "Frustrate their knavish tricks," and "Long may she reign."

Another anonymous text found in Billings ("Th' Eternal speaks") has a meter similar to "My country, 'tis of thee," but with every line longer by a foot than in our National Hymn, thus: 8868886. In it, however, the lines are definitely iambic. James Relly has contributed a genuine dactylic text, which should be given complete:

> Jesus, thy name we praise!
> To thee our songs we raise!
>   Hail! holy Lamb;
> Thou hast redeemed us,
> Greatly esteemed us,
> Witness thy sacrifice, torment, and shame.

The meter is 6 6 4 5 5 10, and the poet has carefully followed it through ten stanzas.

Two of James Relly's iambic poems go so far beyond most English verse in intricacy of structure that they may be properly compared with the astounding stanzas of 15th and 16th century German poetry. An excellent example of the latter is "Ach, Jupiter," a text which had appeared as early as 1519 and is set by Ludwig Senfl in Ott's collection of 1544. Entirely iambic, the syllable and rhyme scheme is as follows:

8 4 8 8 4 8 2 2 4 2 6 2 2 4 2 6 4 4 8
a a b a a b c c d d e f f g g e h h

This nominally has twelve lines, but internal rhyme extends it to nineteen.

Now consider Relly:

Greatly beloved,	Of God approved
Ere time began	Jehovah's darling, man,
Possessed his nature, love,	Above.
There man is known	Whilst angels own
Above them far	This bright and morning star.

This meter, 4446624446, rhyming in couplets throughout, has been followed through eight stanzas.

The second Relly poem has an even longer stanza:

O how doth God our souls surprise
When he our conscience doth baptise
Into the holy nature.
Where free from all offense and blame
We now possess in Christ the Lamb
The fulness of his stature.

Now free	Are we
And shall ever	In our Savior
Stand perfected	With him to this grace elected.

Here the meter is:

8 8 7 8 8 7 2 2 4 4 4 8
a a b c c b d d e e f f

Note in both Relly stanzas the presence of the monometric line, which added greatly to the difficulty of writing the "Ach, Jupiter" stanza also.

One can understand why Billings became interested in the striking Relly meters shown above and on previous pages, since they offer such rich possibilities for asymmetry in melody. We can be very grateful to both poet and composer for the happy combination of text and tune which was the result.

The texts for Billings' anthems present wholly different prob-

lems from those associated with the psalm tunes. A fair proportion of the anthem texts consist of the metrical translations of
Tate and Brady and the psalms and hymns of Isaac Watts. Pope's
"Vital spark" also occurs, and one anthem is based partly on the
blank verse of Young's *Night Thoughts*. However, only four
Billings anthems from more than forty examined had metrical
texts exclusively, and the subject of particular meters does not
become involved at all.

The majority of the anthem texts have been taken directly
from a prose version of the *Book of Psalms*, thirty-seven different psalms having been utilized, with individual excerpts varying
from a single verse to ten or more. But fourteen other books
of the Old Testament also yielded texts, including eight different
chapters of *Isaiah* and six of *Jeremiah*. Four anthems are based
on the *Song of Solomon*, "Sanctify a fast" consists of eleven
verses from the first and second chapters of *Joel*, and "The beauty
of Israel" has been drawn from the first chapter of *II Samuel*.

In most cases the psalm texts are from the Authorized Version
(King James), *Psalms 19, 60*, and *126* in the *Continental Har-
mony* being examples. But Billings was also familiar with the
Church of England Psalter (Prayer Book) and drew *Psalms 39,
65, 81*, and *133* entirely from this source. Sometimes he would
pick words and phrases impartially from both versions, as in
"Sing praises to the Lord." This is a short anthem based on
Psalm 30, its opening verse being verse 4 of the Psalter. Here is
Billings' version of the first part of verse 5: "For his wrath endures but a moment, and in his favor is life evermore." Here
"wrath" is Psalter, "moment" and "favor" are Authorized Version, "forevermore" is Billings' addition, and "endures" is one
of the not uncommon instances of Billings' failure to maintain
the solemn style. Then in the remainder of verse 5, concluding
the anthem, the word "heaviness" is also Psalter.

Often the departures from standard texts show considerable
imagination, as in verse 3 of *Psalm 148*, where the Authorized
Version and Psalter have "stars of light" and "stars and light"
respectively, but Billings says "blazing comets." Moreover, Billings is to a considerable extent his own psalmist. In verse 1 of the
same psalm, to the phrase "to praise him in the heights" he adds
"praise him in the depth." After verse 5 he has the adjuration:

"Admire, adore." Verse 11 has a considerable addition: "Jew and gentile, male and female, bond and free, earth and heaven, land and water, praise the Lord." The next verse should read: "Both young men and maidens; old men and children." Billings gives it delightfully modern overtones with his "Young men and maids; old men and babes." He then breaks into doggerel verse of his own composition: "Join creation, preservation, and redemption, join in one. No exemption, nor dissension, one invention, and intention, reigns through the whole, to praise the Lord." To this he tacks on "Hallelujah, praise the Lord," following the example of his English contemporaries, where the standard conclusion was "Hallelujah, amen."

Billings' *Universal Praise* begins with the first verse of the Psalter version of Psalm 150: "O praise God, praise him in his holiness." It continues with the most delightful of Billings' original couplets: "Praise him propagation; praise him, vegetation," with the further trope, "and let your voice proclaim your choice and testify to standers-by with ardent fire your firm desire to praise the Lord. Let the leading bass inspire, let the tenor catch the fire, let the counter still be higher, let the treble join the choir." (Of course the several voices enter in the order indicated.) The remainder of the anthem consists of a metrical version of portions of Psalms 148, 149, and 150, well mixed together.

Two of Billings' patriotic anthems contain very interesting texts. *Retrospect* begins like a letter from the front line: "Was not the day dark and gloomy! The enemy said, 'Let us draw a line even from York to Canada.' But, praised be the Lord!, the snare is broken and we are escaped." In the course of this anthem Billings draws upon three different chapters of *Jeremiah:* Chapter 48: 10 ("Cursed be the man . . ."), Chapter 4: 19 ("My bowels; I am pained . . .") and Chapter 47: 6 ("O thou sword of the Lord"). From *Isaiah* come "Beat your swords into plowshares . . ." (Chapter 2: 4) and "How beautiful upon the mountains . . . that publisheth peace." (Chapter 52: 7) In quodlibet fashion Billings has joined this verse to the New Testament's "Peace be on earth, goodwill to men," (*Luke* 2: 4) followed by "Hallelujah, for the Lord God omnipotent reigneth." (*Revelation* 19:6)

The most famous of Billings' patriotic anthems is his *Lamentation Over Boston*. Its beginning is a paraphrase of Psalm 137: "By the rivers of Watertown we sat down and wept. We wept when we remembered thee, O Boston." "Babylon" and "Zion" are in the Bible text. A little later occurs one of the most striking of all Billingsisms: "Forbid it, Lord God, that those who have sucked Bostonian breasts should thirst for American blood." Then comes, "A voice was heard in Roxbury which echoed through the continent weeping for Boston because of their danger." This stems from *Jeremiah* 3: 21: "A voice was heard upon the high places . . . ." The following verse is also based upon *Jeremiah*, being a parody rather than a paraphrase of Chapter 31: 20: "Is Boston my dear town? is it my native place? for since their calamity I do earnestly remember it still." The original reads: "Is Ephraim my dear son? is he a pleasant child? for since I spake against him, I do earnestly remember him still."

Other patriotic anthems are "The states, O Lord" and "Be glad, then, America." Billings' patriotic hymn, *Chester*, is often cited as a flagrant example of Billings' chauvinism, as he declares in the first stanza: "We trust in God: New England's God forever reigns." However, this is no more provincial than Isaac Watts's paraphrase of Psalm 100: "Sing to the Lord with joyful voice. Let every land his name adore. The British Isles shall send the noise Across the ocean to the shore."

Billings' already noted combination of texts from most widely separated parts of the Scriptures betrays a truly comprehensive, if not always profound, knowledge of the Bible. Sometimes the sources are indicated, as in the Charity Anthem, "Blessed is he that considereth the poor." Here Billings tells us correctly that the text has been taken from *Matthew*, Chapters 5 and 25; *I Corinthians*, Chapters 13 and 14, and *Psalms* 34 and 41.

Sometimes he is more cryptic: "Words from Tate and Brady, Scripture, etc.," as in the heading for his Ordination Anthem, "O thou to whom all creatures bow,"—the first verse of the New Version of Psalm 8. A second rhymed excerpt comes later, as well as texts from eight other sources, including the Sanctus ("Glory be to thee, O Lord"). As in the anthem *Retrospect*, Billings has a quodlibet juxtaposition of the verses from *Isaiah* and *Luke* which dovetail on the word "peace." Here there is a second quodlibet,

as he combines Psalm 115: 1 with the same verse from *Luke.*
"not unto us, O Lord, but unto thy name be the glory. Glory be
to God on high, peace be on earth."

More often Billings says: "An anthem taken from sundry
scriptures," as in his "Who is this that cometh from Edom, with
dyed garments from Bozrah?" (*Isaiah* 63: 1) He follows this
question with a typical Billings trope ("Who is he and what's his
name?") as a bridge to ten further scriptural texts and para-
phrases: "His name shall be called wonderful Counselor, the
mighty God, the everlasting Father, the Prince of Peace (*Isaiah*
9: 6); the great I AM (*Exodus* 3: 14); the first and last, the Alpha
and Omega (*Revelation* 1: 11; *cf. Isaiah* 41: 4) Shiloh (*Genesis*
49: 10); Emanuel, God with us (*Isaiah* 7: 14); the Lord our
righteousness (*Jeremiah* 23: 6); the seed of the woman, serpent
bruiser (*Genesis* 3: 15); Lamb of God (*John* 1: 29); equal with
the Father (*John* 5: 18; *cf. Philippians* 2: 6); mercy and truth
have met together; righteousness and peace have kissed each
other (Psalm 85: 10)." The anthem concludes with an extended
metrical text on the crucifixion.

Even when Billings announces a particular psalm as the sole
source for his text, there is no assurance that it will not draw
more heavily from other sources. A case in point is the anthem
called "*Psalm 44th.* Suitable to be sung on the anniversary of our
forefathers' landing and for Thanksgiving." True, its first five
verses do come from Psalm 44, but then in rapid succession come
verses from a dozen other sources: Psalm 11, *Luke* 15, *I Kings*
8, *II Corinthians* 1, Psalm 68, Psalm 45, Psalm 100, *Exodus* 15,
Psalm 146, Psalm 45, and *Deuteronomy* 27. The reference from
Luke is a paraphrase of the cry of the Prodigal Son: "O Lord, we
acknowledge that we have sinned and are not worthy to be called
thy children." The original of *Exodus* 15: 9 reads: "The enemy
said . . . I will draw my sword, my hand shall destroy them."
But Billings, as much at home with Hebraic parallelism as was the
author of *Exodus,* has strengthened the phraseology to read:
"The enemy said I will brandish my sword, I will flourish my
sword: my hand shall demolish them, my hand shall devour
them."

With the above choice example of Billings the psalmist we
conclude our study of Billings' texts. Can this be the same

William Billings whom many short-sighted critics have dismissed as ignorant and crude? The true Billings deserves our respect. We have seen that the texts for his psalm tunes form a first-rate anthology of 18th century religious poetry, well furbished with interesting particular meters, including the intricate stanzas of the Relly brothers. For his anthems he was equally skilled at choosing texts, and at times had what amounted to a genius at constructing them, an act of creation and synthesis in which he far excelled his colleagues on either side of the Atlantic.

Rhythm and Meter

One of the most persistent, but totally false, allegations among Billings' critics is that in setting his texts he was often guilty of poor prosody—a charge which many an excellent composer, Schubert, for example, has not escaped. Macdougall[8] says: "His feeling for the proper adaptation of the musical rhythm to the poetical meter was also at times ludicrously lacking." Daniel, whose approach to Billings is very sympathetic, quotes Billings' own attitude about prosody to the effect that "where the sense and the sound run counter to each other, the sound must give way."[9] This is a true statement of Billings' practice, but is the exact opposite of sacrificing a text to musical exigencies! Daniel goes on to say that Billings failed "to understand the basic principles of metric organization" and thus became guilty of "metric awkwardness," especially in the earlier period. This is too sweeping a charge, and it by no means applies solely to Billings, as we shall see.

We do find in Billings and his contemporaries a fairly large number of wrong metrical signatures. These are errors indeed, and no attempt will be made to gloss over them. But, in all but a negligible number of cases, the composers have not been guilty of poor prosody; they have simply failed to notate their intended rhythms as clearly as possible. This is especially true of free rhythms, which Billings almost always did clarify by changing signatures, but which his contemporaries signally failed so to indicate. Many of our contemporary composers, caught between the Scylla of the desire for great rhythmic freedom and the Charybdis of difficulty of performance with constantly changing signatures, have preferred to maintain a conventional signature, with rhythmic nuances shown by marks of accent. This was what most of the American and minor English com-

[8] *Op. cit.*, p. 161.
[9] Daniel, *op. cit.*, p. 193.

posers of the 18th century did, except that it was unnecessary for them to add the accent marks, since the words were an indication of how the accents should fall.

The baldest sort of error—and the rarest—was to have the metrical signature correct, but to have the barline shifted. If the signature itself is wrong, there will be frequent points of coincidence between the real and the indicated accents. But, with shifted barline, all the accents will be wrong. There are, however, degrees of error even here, of which the worst is $\frac{4}{4}$ with the barline shifted one beat. In Billings' *Lebanon* (Example 1) the

barline is wrongly placed except in the fourth phrase. (Unless otherwise indicated, a single melodic line in the examples is the tenor part.) *Lebanon* appeared originally in NEPS; in SMA the errors have all been corrected, as shown above the first notation—the time values of the second and third notes have been halved, the cadential note of the second phrase has been lengthened, and the first note of the final phrase has been shortened. The revised version is in A minor, with $\frac{2}{2}$ meter; it retains the Aeolian feeling in the tenor, but three sharped leading notes occur in the soprano which were not present before.

A less heinous error in duple meter is for the barline to be shifted by two beats, for primary and secondary accents are not always clearly differentiated. Composers like Schumann have been guilty of such errors on a grand scale, so why should the naïve tunesmiths be blamed if they sin occasionally? But this too was a very rare error among the psalm composers. Only one instance was located in Billings (Example 2): the first phrase of his *Old South* begins correctly enough; but the three-note mel-

isma on the fourth syllable causes the halfnotes to be accented incorrectly. This throws off all the accents in the second phrase, where the half note is the unit. The third phrase is rhythmically similar to the first, but the shifted barline is not correct. In the fourth phrase the melisma has four notes and the following note is lengthened to two beats, so that there is a pleasant feeling of syncopation and a broadened cadence, but no false accents. It is easy to correct this example: begin the tune on the downbeat, and lengthen the cadential note of the second phrase to a whole note!

There are also a few examples in Arnold of shifted barlines in duple meter, the most interesting of which is in *Thrussington*. Example 3 shows two phrases in $\frac{2}{2}$ meter, the latter of which is

correct, whereas the former has two wrongly placed accents. But the passage has not been put in its proper context: it is preceded by eighteen bars of $\frac{3}{2}$ and followed by nine more bars of $\frac{2}{2}$. The probable solution is to have the $\frac{3}{2}$ continue for two bars longer, *i.e.*, for the duration of the first phrase shown; the accents are then correct.

The beginning of this same Arnold tune is in triple meter, but

there is a momentary shift of accent at the end of Example 4.
Here no simpler solution suggests itself than to add a beat to the

fifth bar, thus shifting the barline one beat to the right, for the
remainder of the example.

A very interesting shift of accent in triple meter occurs in the
fuguing tune, *Derby*, found in Adams. There are two fugues in
the first part, with correct accentuation throughout except that
the penultimate bar should have four beats. This throws off the
accent in the final bar, as may be seen in the soprano part in
Example 5a. Thus the fugue which begins the second part

should have the barline one beat to the right, and all four voices
enter in accordance with the shifted barline. (Example 5b).

But, as the voices again enter fugally after a bar's rest, the accent agrees with the barring, and there is a charming rhythmic clash between the new entries of soprano and alto, with the end of the old phrase in tenor and bass. The suggested emendation of the metric scheme includes one bar of $\frac{5}{4}$ in each voice.

More common than the shift of barline in duple or triple meter was the use of the wrong metrical signature, especially of $\frac{2}{2}$ in place of $\frac{3}{2}$ Billings has a clear example in the Long Meter tune *Stockbridge.* (Example 6) Here three stanzas of the text are set with different music, the error in notation occurring only in the first. There are six phrases in Billings' setting of this stanza, the first four being solos with added bass, and the remaining two being a choral reply set to the text of the third and fourth lines. The rhythm of the first three phrases demands a $\frac{3}{2}$ signature; in

the fourth phrase a slight change in the position of the paired quarters and halves has made the music fit the $\frac{2}{2}$ signature. Note that the rhythm of this fourth phrase is that of the older version of *Old Hundredth*, as frequently printed in modern hymnals.

The wrongly notated rhythm of the L.M. tune *Stockbridge* was also often found in C.M. tunes, as throughout Billings' *North River* (Example 7). But, although it is possible to correct a L.M.

tune just by changing the signature and the barlines, this does not work so well with the shorter second and fourth phrases of a C.M. tune. If the cadential note of Billings' second phrase is lengthened to a whole note (a desirable change in any case) the triple meter is maintained without break.

If the poetic meter 6666 had been in use in 18th century

psalmody, it would not matter whether the rhythmic motive occurring in the above Billings tunes had been used with a duple or a triple signature, for the accents fall equally well for a duple measure beginning on the downbeat as for a triple measure beginning on the third beat. The closest approach to this four-line stanza is Short Meter, 6686. In the S.M. tune *Wirksworth*, printed in Lyon, the first two phrases are correct as they stand. (Example 8) In the third phrase the accents are thrown off be-

cause of the superfluous half rest at the beginning of the phrase to allow for a lengthened cadential note. If the rest is removed and the cadential note made a half note, the ambiguous $\frac{2}{2}$, $\frac{3}{2}$ will run consistently through the entire tune. The revised barring for the third phrase with $\frac{2}{2}$ signature is shown beneath the music. Example 7, as amended, would also be satisfactory with a $\frac{2}{2}$ signature if the barline were shifted one beat to the left. Such a shift would also serve well for the first three phrases of Example 6, but would be wrong for the fourth phrase unless a bar of $\frac{3}{2}$ were to be included. The rhythm in the above three tunes was extremely common in the 18th century.

Billings' *Europe* is another wrongly notated C.M. tune, although its rhythm is by no means ambiguous. (Example 9) As

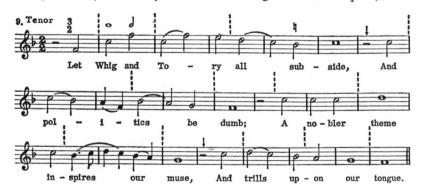

printed in NEPS with a ${}^2_2$ signature, there are at least four mis-placed accents. In MM, Billings has corrected the tune as shown above the music, by changing the signature to ${}^3_2$, lengthening the second note to a whole note, and removing two rests. He also confirmed the modulation to the dominant key at the end of the first phrase by inserting the needed natural before B flat.

Although wrongly notated triple meter occurred most fre-quently in settings of iambic stanzas, that was only because they were so much more common than trochaic stanzas. At least one trochaic tune, *Ashfield*, found in Shumway, used a rhythmic motive very similar to that shown in several examples above, and was in similar need of a triple signature. (Example 10) The

composer's failure to observe the intended elision in "th' arch-angel's" has done some slight violence to the verse in phrases three and five. If the first three notes of the third phrase are halved and the rest at the end of the second phrase deleted, the entire tune falls into a triple pattern. A piquant effect arises from the patter rhythm in the repetition of lines three and four. In the original, the part shown is followed by a fuguing refrain which is wholly duple.

Examples of wrongly barred triple meter are much rarer among the anthems. A difficult passage to construe occurs in the F major section of Billings' "The beauty of Israel is slain."

(Example 11) Here so much of the melody falls naturally into a
$\frac{3}{2}$ meter that Billings may have wanted triple meter for the entire

Let the daugh-ters of the Phi - lis - tines re - joice,   re - joice,

should re - joice   and the daugh-ters of the un-cir-cum-ciz-èd tri-

umph, tri-umph, tri-umph, and the daugh-ters of the un-cir-cum-siz-èd tri-umph.

passage, but lacked the skill to notate it. With a few Procrustean
changes—the omission of the two rests, the shortening of one
note and the lengthening of another—the triple nature of the
meter is preserved throughout. Note that the three "triumphs"
now appear as two bars in $\frac{3}{2}$ meter, with the delightful syncopated
effect so common in the minuets of Lully and Purcell. It must
be admitted that Billings' melody is not up to its usual level in
this passage, no matter how it is barred.

Duple meter barred as triple also occurs in Billings' anthems.
An especially good instance of such metrical conflict occurs in
"The Lord is King," the first anthem of his first collection. Here
an entire section of twenty-five bars in $\frac{3}{4}$ meter should actually be
in duple meter. Example 12 contains bars 14-19 of this passage.

The Lord on high is migh-tier than the noise of man-y wa-ters.

When the signature is changed to $\frac{4}{4}$ retaining $\frac{3}{4}$ only for the bar
with the word "waters," the accents fall into place.

The English composers also sometimes failed to indicate the

correct meter, as in Example 13 from Williams' anthem, *Psalm 122*, where a $\frac{4}{4}$ signature at the beginning of the second full bar is

needed if "sense" and "sound" (to use Billings' terminology) are to coincide. The half note on "shall" in the first bar, a familiar sarabande motive, will not be stressed too much, just like the last "triumph" in Example 11.

A virtually unique instance of actual false prosody in Billings, combined with wrong barring, is found in "Hear my prayer." (Example 14) This anthem is not free from rhythmic nuances

of a legitimate nature, but in the passage quoted the duple meter strongly demanded by melodic rhythm creates four false accents. Even this horrible example can be salvaged, if one desires, by a slight change in underlaying the text: remove the slur over the quarter notes at the beginning of the second bar and extend the slur in the final bar to include the preceding half note. (Example 14a)

One example of an incorrect triple signature in a psalm tune should be sufficient, from the fuguing Chorus of Tans'ur's

Uppingham. (Example 15) The responsive first part of this tune, not shown here, fits the $\frac{3}{4}$ signature perfectly; the fuguing part is emphatically duple, even to the entry of each voice after four beats; the triple meter asserts itself again only at the end.

In the anthems, especially, there was often a broadening of the

rhythm at a cadence, indicated by longer note values rather than by a retard. This is shown smoothly and normally in a cadence from Williams' *Psalm 122* (Example 16), where the meter is

already triple and the half note on "thee" falls into the sarabande rhythm noted in Example 13 in this same anthem. But when the meter is duple, the broadening of the cadence often results in an actual triple meter which runs counter to the metrical signature. For example, Billings' *David's Lamentation* ends with the words, "O Absalom, my son, my son." (Example 17) As notated, the

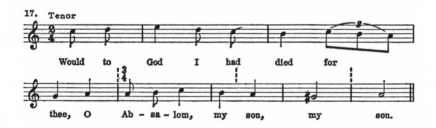

word "my" twice receives a superfluous accent. But if a $\frac{3}{4}$ signature is placed after the third full bar, the principal stress is thrown upon "son," where it belongs.

There is a similar cadence in Tans'ur's *Psalm 47* (Example 18), where the change to $\frac{3}{4}$ at the third bar eliminates the ugly

syncopation on the word "earth," as well as the over-stress on "the." Billings matches this example with an *alla breve* instance in his "Sing ye merrily," with a $\frac{3}{2}$ signature to be assumed at the beginning of the example. (Example 19)

In Daniel Read's "O be joyful in the Lord," the passage shown (Example 20) makes musical sense as it stands, but there is a

strong accent on the article "a." Here at last is a passage that might provide ammunition for the snipers! If "singing" is substituted for "a song," the prosody becomes perfect. However, Read did not intend this effect. If a $\frac{3}{4}$ signature is inserted at the beginning of the fourth bar, the penultimate bar becomes identical with that in the Williams and revised Tans'ur examples. (Examples 16 and 18)

Billings' "By the rivers of Watertown" contains a more complex rhythmic feature. (Example 21) At the beginning of this

passage, the rhythmic unit is the quarter note. This changes to a half-note beat at the beginning of the third bar. But, simultaneously, there is a broadening to a triple meter in approaching the cadence. So a signature of $\frac{3}{2}$ is needed at the third bar, to make the cadence effective.

An even subtler relation crops up in Billings' "Samuel the priest." (Example 22) Here there is no question of implied

triple meter. But the whole note on "the" seems as false as the half-note "a" in Example 20. The solution here is to assume a signature of $\frac{4}{2}$ at the beginning of the first full measure, thus subordinating "the" to "name" and "Lord."

An extension of the idea of cadential broadening, together with an incorrect metrical signature, is to be found at the beginning of Billings' hymn anthem, "The Lord descended from above." (Example 23) Obviously, a signature of $\frac{4}{4}$ is needed up to the bar where the melisma on "darkness" begins; from there on, the $\frac{3}{4}$ barring is correct.

Later in this same anthem (Example 24) occurs one of the most unusual instances of metrical subtlety in Billings or any

of his contemporaries. Here, as in the previous example, the signature makes no sense. A $\frac{2}{2}$ signature at the beginning of the

triplet quarters turns the first part of the passage into a virtual
$\frac{6}{4}$, but not of the courante type in which a $\frac{3}{2}$ may have an alterna-
tive accentuation. However, with the dropping of the triplets
at the beginning of the word "darkness," the soprano melody
does fit the courante type of $\frac{6}{4}$ Then, in the following bar, especially in the soprano part, there is momentarily an impression
that the whole note has become the rhythmic unit, since the
four quarters become collectively the accented beat. (All this,
of course, is within the general framework of a $\frac{2}{2}$ signature!) So
the original beat has become two-thirds as fast and then half as
fast; as it takes on its first value again in the final bar, one may
surely assume a retard.

Sometimes the alternation between duple and triple meter
occurs so regularly that adjacent bars tend to combine to form
such additive meters as $\frac{5}{4}$ or $\frac{7}{4}$. The occurrence of $\frac{5}{4}$ in a polyphonic
setting has already been observed in Example 5b. Benjamin
West has an especially lovely instance of $\frac{5}{4}$ in his anthem, "O clap
your hands," as Daniel has noted. (Example 25) Here the motive

on "O sing praises" consists of five quarters, and it is carried
through four times—five times, if the rest is omitted at the end
of the passage. In the shorter answering phrase, the accents fall
into a $\frac{6}{4}$ pattern. A passage in West's, "O Lord our governor,"
also has a predominant quintuple meter, with a bar of $\frac{7}{4}$ in the
exact middle of the phrase. (Example 26)

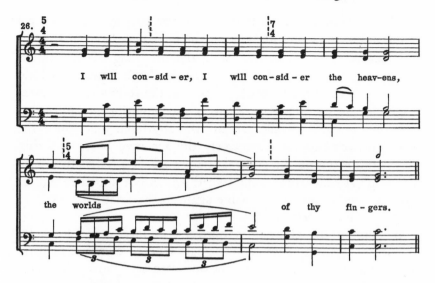

A short interchange between alto and tenor in Stephenson's Christmas anthem, "Behold, I bring you," gives a clear and convincing example of $\frac{7}{4}$ ($\frac{3}{4}$ plus $\frac{4}{4}$). (Example 27) There is also an incidental passage of $\frac{7}{4}$ in Arnold's "O sing unto the Lord."

Relatively clear, but far from convincing, is the fuguing Chorus from Tans'ur's psalm tune *Dorchester*, a setting of Psalm 33. (Example 28) Here the entries are stiltedly regular and uninteresting. The meter will be perceived to be $\frac{5}{4}$ until the slight broadening to $\frac{6}{4}$ at the cadence.

More examples of completely free rhythm—always wrongly barred—can be found in Tans'ur than in any other composer, English or American, whose church music was published in America during the 18th century. He was, of course, attempting to catch the rhythms of speech. It is easy, but incorrect, to say that such free rhythms have their roots in Gregorian chant. Although irregularity of rhythm is an earmark of plainsong, most chants are too florid to have much connection with speech

rhythms, and no connection whatever with English speech rhythms. In any case, Protestants in England and New England would have been only remotely influenced by any music of the Roman Catholic Church, but would have been strongly influenced by the music of the Church of England. The free

rhythms of the Anglican chant made an impression upon mem-
bers of the established church and dissenters alike. The benedic-
tion of Billings' "I love the Lord," for example, is so chantlike
that it might have come direct from Merbecke. (Example 29)

An especially effective example of Tans'ur's free rhythm is
found in his anthem, *Psalm 148*. (Example 30) In this little

duet for tenor and bass there is a natural flow of melody, the
duple and triple measures being almost equally balanced, with
triple predominating at the beginning and duple toward the end.
The bass solo in his *Psalm 104* (Example 31) is equally free, and

has a good melody, marred only by the slight floridity in "of the wind." (The same motive is satisfactory in "feedeth them.") In this passage the vocal bass is supported by an organ continuo line, which faithfully follows the quadruple meter of the signature, except at the cadence. This poses a knotty problem of attempting to reconcile melodic with harmonic rhythm, comparable to that of the organist who has to provide a modal accompaniment to plainsong. Of course, in New England the passage would probably have been sung unaccompanied, thus cutting the knot.

Aaron Williams has given in *Wells* a tune whose irregular rhythm is maintained throughout, with something of the freedom of the earliest French and English psalm tunes. (Example 32) There is neither text nor psalm heading, but, with eight

notes in each phrase, the meter is almost surely L.M. If so, the accents are a bit tricky, for the pattern of two quarters and a half in the third bar must be treated differently from the same pattern in the second bar. A possible solution, shown above the music, is to omit the rests and to have two bars of $\frac{3}{4}$ in the middle of each phrase.

With the possible exception of Williams' *Wells*, all of the examples of wrongly barred free meter given so far are sufficiently clear that the error in notation would have caused no trouble in performance. The tune *Barnstable*, found in Read, is more exasperating. (Example 33) The meter is 7s Dbl, and the second half is as regular as the ticking of a clock. In the first half, however, each of the first three phrases contains nine beats, divided as follows: 3 2 4; 4 3 2; 4 3 2. The fourth phrase might have

been stronger if it too had had the 4 3 2 pattern, curtailed, however, by the demands of the signature. (If the tune had begun
on the downbeat, two more beats would have been available at
the end of the fourth phrase.) The fifth phrase, not shown in the
example, is identical with the first phrase save for its initial note;
this note being only one beat long, the phrase fits two bars of
common time perfectly. The melody as a whole is by no means
unpleasing; without frequent changes of signature its beauties are
hidden indeed.

In Arnold a troublesome tune is *Garenton,* a setting of verses
10-13 of Psalm 90 Old Version. Only the first and second phrases
are irregular in their rhythm, with an implied pattern (2 2 3 3 2;
3 3 2 2 2) in which the strong accent coincides with the beginning
of the bar in only two places. The second phrase is interesting:
the word "threescore," normally a spondee, is strongly trochaic
in its context. As set, however, the spondaic nature of the word
is preserved, although "fourscore" in the third phrase is set as
a trochee. (Example 34)

Billings, although prone to use an incorrect signature for a passage in a definite meter, was careful about notating free rhythms, especially in his anthems, with their prose texts. One of the rare exceptions is a tenor solo in "The Lord is King." (Example 35) In both phrases of the balanced period, the real meter is chiefly duple, with one bar of $\frac{3}{4}$ interspersed.

In his settings of metrical psalms, Billings was not quite so meticulous about changing the signature to fit the rhythm, probably because the poetical accents were sufficient clue to the accentuation. An extreme example is the tune, *Ashford*. (Example 36) It begins with the triple meter indicated by the signature. The next three phrases are duple, with a broadening cadence in the fourth phrase; the fifth phrase is triple, and the sixth again is duple. In this responsive L.M. tune with Chorus the melody flows so naturally, always matching the accents of the text, that the lack of correspondence between the metrical signature and the needed accents is no deterrent to the singer.

A curious example of free rhythm, barred both incorrectly and correctly, occurs in Billings' anthem, "We have heard with our ears." (Example 37) At the beginning of the passage, for which the $\frac{2}{2}$ signature is largely correct, the true rhythm calls for a bar of $\frac{3}{2}$, without which the remaining four accents are misplaced. Then another implied $\frac{3}{2}$ bar makes the accents fall properly in the remaining three bars. In the expansion of this lovely passage which follows therewith, Billings has changed the meter six times from duple to triple and back again, with perfect accentuation.

One of the most admirable features of Billings' writing is that he usually did change the metrical signature to correspond to

Chorus

The shep – herd by whose con – stant

care My wants are all sup – plied.

37.

hear us from heav'n and when thou hear'st, for – give,

and when thou hear'st for – give. Fa – ther of

mer-cy, God of con - so - la - tion, hear us, hear from

heav'n, thy dwell – ing place, and when thou hear'st, for –

give, and when thou hear'st, for – give.

the true meter, as in the latter part of the above example. The English composers with whose works he was familiar almost never did this. A single exception was located in an anthem, Knapp's "Unto us a child is born" (Example 38), where in a duet for tenor and bass the meter shifts smoothly from $\frac{2}{2}$ to $\frac{3}{2}$.

A few instances of correctly changing signatures may be found in the psalm tunes written by Billings' contemporaries. Two good examples are to be found in Arnold. In the tune *Loughborough* the voices shift easily from a two- to a three-beat in approaching a cadence. (Example 39) There is a similarly

smooth shift in the alto part in the first six bars of Arnold's *Hathorne*.

The anthems of all the composers studied had many changes of metrical signature, marking off the major divisions of the work. Although the psalm tunes were usually so short that no sections were present, there were plenty of double and even triple stanzas among the settings. Here, just as in the anthems, the changed signatures were not uncommon, as in Billings' fuguing tune *Creation*. (See p. 83) Exceptionally, the change of signature came near the final cadence, as in the tune *Sharon*. (Example 40) The C.M. text is clothed with a lively melody in $\frac{6}{4}$ extended to six phrases by repeating the third and fourth lines of the text and then to eight phrases by repeating the music of the extension, and to nine by adding a coda. On the second end-

ing the meter changes to $\frac{3}{2}$. It is evident that the quarter note does not remain constant at the change of meter, for the soprano has the same trumpet-like lilt as before, now written as a triplet. So it is the primary beat which changes from duple to triple, and, there being no further triplets, the dignified coda expresses well the text: "His dreadful majesty."

Another special use of changing signatures was for punctuation. In Billings' psalm tune, *Sunday*, the first three phrases are in $\frac{3}{2}$. (Example 41) The setting of the fourth line of the text is ex-

tended by a fourfold repetition of its opening words, "I'm lost."
(This textual repetition gives a rather amusing and paradoxical
effect, similar to some of the gaucheries found in fuguing pas-
sages.) So a $\frac{2}{2}$ signature (implying $\frac{4}{2}$) is used to provide for the
punctuation, with a return to $\frac{3}{2}$ afterward. In Billings' *Berlin* there
is a similar extension to an implied $\frac{4}{2}$ to punctuate the repeated
phrase, "He dies."

Punctuation played a part in another of the extremely rare instances of indicated metrical shifts among Billings' contemporaries. At the beginning of Shumway's *Wales*, an extra beat is
needed for the punctuating rest after the repeated word,
"mourn." (Example 42) This example illustrates also the use of

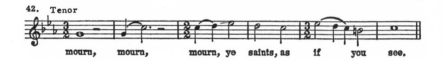

42. Tenor

mourn,   mourn,   mourn, ye saints, as   if   you   see.

changing signatures to provide for ordinary shifts of accent
within a phrase, as the meter shifts back to $\frac{3}{2}$ at the end.

The latter part of Example 37, from Billings' anthem, "We
have heard with our ears," has free rhythm because of the
punctuation. A striking example of punctuation occurs in his
Funeral Anthem, "I heard a great voice," where the pause after
the repeated phrase, "for they rest," gives rise to four bars of
quintuple meter, correctly notated as $\frac{2}{2}$ plus $\frac{3}{2}$. (Example 43)

Another good example of shifting meters occurs in Billings'
early anthem, "Was not the day dark and dreary?" (Example
44) Here there are fifteen bars in $\frac{2}{2}$ meter and only three in $\frac{3}{2}$. In
the concluding Hallelujah of this anthem (Example 45), which
follows the preceding example directly, there is a different

43.   Tenor

Yea,   saith the spir - it,   for   they   rest,   for   they

rest,   for they   rest,   for   they   rest.

variety of rhythmic shift in addition to the triple-duple shift. In a $\frac{3}{2}$ meter in Billings' day there would theoretically be 60 half notes per minute, but in a $\frac{3}{4}$ meter, 90. So the shift from $\frac{3}{2}$ to $\frac{3}{4}$ represents a speeding up of the tempo by half, and the return to $\frac{3}{2}$ at the end corresponds to the conventional retard that was never indicated by words.

To sum up this lengthy discussion on rhythm: in the vast majority of cases, Billings and the other composers of psalm tunes used one metrical signature for the entire tune, and the rhythm of the tune conformed strictly to the signature. In the anthems the use of several signatures was common and it was not rare in the psalm tunes, but almost always to mark off major divisions. A very rare use of changing signatures in both anthems and psalm tunes was for punctuation of a repeated word or short phrase. Just as rare was their use to indicate free rhythms within a phrase; but more frequently these charming internal shifts in the primary accent were not marked by a corresponding change in the signature. Billings was an exception to this slovenly custom, being the only one of these composers to indicate free rhythms by changing signatures with any degree of consistency. And, although false barring was generally prevalent, false prosody (the ridiculous charge leveled by present-day critics) was virtually non-existent.

Melody

Billings' greatest asset was his unerring feeling for melody, which is evident everywhere in his anthems. Often the melody is of the simplest and most regular type, as in the beginning of "We have heard with our ears," with its smooth setting of anapests. (Example 46) At the risk of being called a Spaetheist,

46. Tenor.

We have heard with our ears and our fa-thers have told us.

I note that in the anthem "Is any afflicted" there is a tenor phrase identical with "London Bridge is falling down." (Example 47)

47. Tenor

teach – ing and ad – mon – ish – ing

This can be matched in "O thou to whom," where "The farmer in the dell" yields to the sixth phrase of "Columbia, the gem of the ocean." (Example 48) Just as folklike, but with more modern

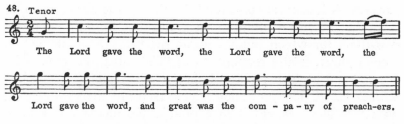

48. Tenor

The Lord gave the word, the Lord gave the word, the

Lord gave the word, and great was the com – pa – ny of preach-ers.

connotations, is Example 49, from the Communion Anthem, "Let

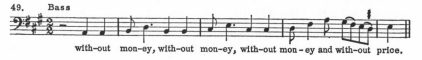

49. Bass

with-out mon-ey, with-out mon-ey, with-out mon-ey and with-out price.

every mortal ear attend," in which "Ol' Man River" is plainly heard.

The repeated text in the previous examples is one of Billings' characteristics. He likes to state the first part of a sentence three times and then complete it, thus getting a well-rounded phrase. Another example of this tendency, of which scores of examples could be cited from the anthems, is from his second setting of the text, "Blessed is he." (Example 50) Note that the first motive

50. Tenor

and to keep him-self un - spot-ted, to keep him-self un -

spot-ted, to keep him-self un - spot - ted from the world.

(it is identical with part of the second subject of the first movement of the *New World Symphony*) is then repeated a fourth higher, but is varied considerably upon its second repetition. The passage ends with "Three blind mice," which has also been "found" in the *New World Symphony*, but which is a universal motive.

Paradoxically, Billings seemed to be restricted by the meter of the psalm texts rather than helped by it; and, whereas the melody to prose texts in the anthems, especially in the short solos, was almost always extremely apt, similar passages in the psalm tunes were more likely to fall into somewhat conventional melodic patterns. A folk style comparable to that in the above examples from the anthems is found in the psalm tune *Boston*, one of the two tunes for which Billings wrote the text. (Example 51) Its second phrase is also reminiscent of "Columbia, the gem of the ocean," and its fifth phrase of the Gloria refrain of the *Westminster Carol*. The prevailing iambic meter of the 18th-century texts was likely to result in a bourée-like melody, this being especially noticeable in the typical fuguing pattern for which *Lenox* provided the model. (See Example 103) The meter for *Boston* is C.M. Dbl. Of the eight phrases, the first, fifth, and seventh commence with half notes and the other five phrases with quarters. But the general spirit of the tune is unmistakably

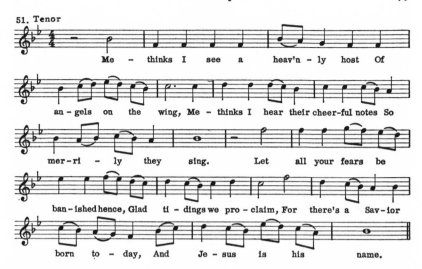

Me - thinks I see a heav'n - ly host Of
an - gels on the wing, Me - thinks I hear their cheer-ful notes So
mer - ri - ly they sing. Let all your fears be
ban - ished hence, Glad ti - dings we pro - claim, For there's a Sav - ior
born to - day, And Je - sus is his name.

that of the bourée rather than that of the gavotte. Observe the repeated quarter notes, and the pairs of eighths, sometimes falling on the strong accent, sometimes on the weak.

The tune *Conquest*, with a trochaic text (8787 with Hallelujah), is set in a very similar dance style; in fact, the group of six eighth notes is identical in the second phrases of both tunes. (Example 52) Here the accented beginnings of the phrases make

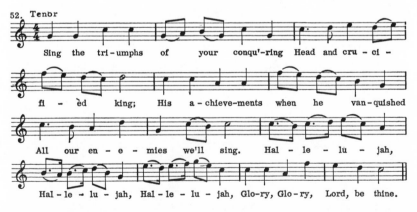

Sing the tri - umphs of your conqu' - ring Head and cru - ci -
fi - ed king; His a - chieve-ments when he van - quished
All our en - e - mies we'll sing. Hal - le - lu - jah,
Hal - le - lu - jah, Hal - le - lu - jah, Glo-ry, Glo-ry, Lord, be thine.

the first part of the tune practically a gavotte. Note that the latter four eighth notes are repeated asymmetrically in the third phrase, but that the dotted quarter and eighth that begin the second phrase are echoed at the beginning of the fourth phrase.

The Hallelujah of Example 52 contains a diminution of the dotted rhythm, with a twofold sequential repetition, the additional Hallelujah pleasingly extending the refrain to five bars. In the first two Hallelujahs there is a suggestion of the fine old English tune, *Greensleeves*. (Example 53) In the 18th-century

53. Soprano

tunes there was a tendency toward *Greensleeves* whenever the progression vi V or ii I occured in a major key with sequential melody, or i VII in a minor key. Billings' anthem, "Let every mortal ear," affords an excellent example. (Example 54) Several

54.

instances are to be found in "By the rivers of Watertown." The anthem *Claremont,* a setting of Pope's "Vital spark," is another rich source of *Greensleeves* reminiscences. (It is printed anonymously in *Southern Harmony*.) The beginning of *Claremont* is shown in Example 55.

55.

Another dance melody is in *Shiloh,* a Christmas carol to the same Billings' text as Example 51. (Example 56) The first part

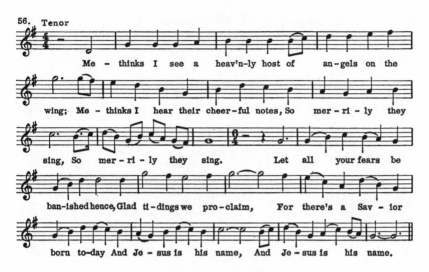

56. Tenor

Me - thinks I see a heav'n-ly host of an-gels on the wing; Me - thinks I hear their cheer-ful notes, So mer - ri - ly they sing, So mer - ri - ly they sing. Let all your fears be ban-ished hence, Glad ti - dings we pro-claim, For there's a Sav - ior born to-day And Je - sus is his name, And Je - sus is his name.

is again in the style of the bourée, with the beginning of the third phrase suggesting *The Girl I Left Behind Me* and, immediately after this, the last phrase of the verse of the *Wassail Song*. Then the meter changes from $\frac{4}{4}$ to $\frac{6}{4}$, with a clever variant of the first melody, although now the first phrase has a lilt like *The Campbells are Coming* and the second like the primordial melody, *Summer is icumen in*.

Most of the dance strains occur with texts that use a triple poetic meter—dactyl, anapest, amphibrach. A familiar example is the Christmas carol, *Judea*, which, like most of the instances, is in amphibrachs. (Example 57) The musical meter is a jiggy $\frac{6}{4}$

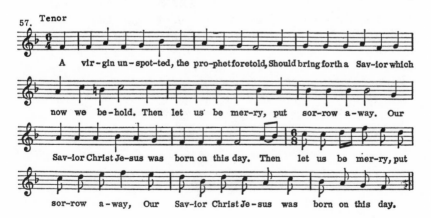

57. Tenor

A vir - gin un - spot-ted, the pro-phet foretold, Should bring forth a Sav-ior which now we be-hold. Then let us be mer-ry, put sor-row a-way. Our Sav-ior Christ Je-sus was born on this day. Then let us be mer-ry, put sor-row a-way, Our Sav-ior Christ Je-sus was born on this day.

which speeds up to $\frac{6}{8}$ in the final phrase. Another carol in the same meter (11s) is *Emanuel*, which, with the chorus, consists of six lines of text. (Example 58) Billings exceptionally used

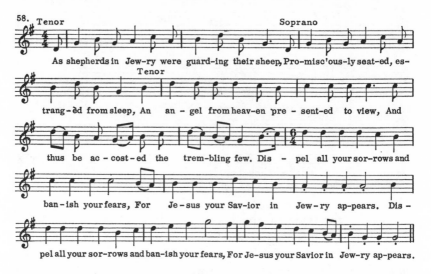

58.

As shepherds in Jew-ry were guard-ing their sheep, Pro-misc'ous-ly seat-ed, es-

trang-èd from sleep, An an - gel from heav-en pre - sent-ed to view, And

thus be ac - cost-ed the trem-bling few. Dis - pel all your sor-rows and

ban-ish your fears, For Je-sus your Sav-ior in Jew-ry ap-pears. Dis -

pel all your sor-rows and ban-ish your fears, For Je-sus your Savior in Jew-ry ap-pears.

duple meter for the verse, changing to triple for the chorus, as in Example 56. The final phrases of the chorus are very similar to the $\frac{6}{8}$ portion of Example 57, with an even more emphatic dance cadence which *cognoscenti* will spot as *Irish Washer-woman*.

Other dancelike $\frac{6}{4}$ tunes by Billings include *Chelsea* (5556 Dbl), *Moravia* (11 11 10 11 11 11), and *Election* (11 66 11 11)—all to texts by Relly, who was skilled indeed at writing in unusual meters. Only one of the texts set by Billings is in dactyls, and this justifies the showing of its tune, *Baltimore*. (Example 59) The

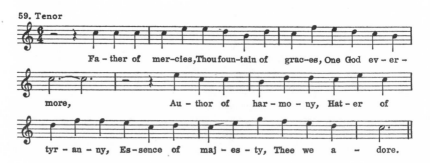

59. Tenor

Fa - ther of mer-cies, Thou foun-tain of grac-es, One God ev - er -

more, Au - thor of har - mo - ny, Hat-er of

tyr - an - ny, Es-sence of maj - es - ty, Thee we a - dore.

very unusual meter is discussed on page 7. Although the style of the text resembles the work of the Relly brothers, the poem is not included in their volume.

It is important to observe that Billings was the only 18th century psalm composer, English or American, to make effective use of dance rhythms in his tunes. It was not until the camp-meeting style crept into printed tunebooks in the early 19th century that the folk element became pronounced in American hymnody, and so Billings must be considered a forerunner rather than a leader in this style.

In Billings' anthems sometimes the most attractive feature is the lack of symmetry, as in his "Was not the day dark and gloomy?" where an antecedent phrase has four and a half bars to only three bars in the consequent phrase, unified by the repetition of a two-bar motive a third lower and the response of the final bar to the first full bar. (Example 60) Even the most dance-

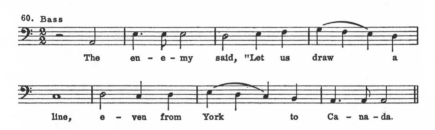

like passage in Billings' anthems (from "Is any afflicted") consists of four plus five bars. (Example 61)

At its best, Billings' melody is fine indeed, as in the plaintive bass solo, "For I am a stranger" (note the implied $\frac{3}{2}$ near the end), from his short anthem, "Hear my prayer." (Example 62) Or the

even more beautiful bass solo, "Now is Christ risen," from the
Easter Anthem, "The Lord is risen indeed." (Example 63) This

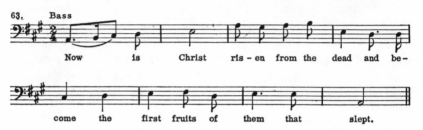

example has plenty of rhythmic variety and only slight motivic
repetition, and yet it is as convincing a setting of this text as has
ever been written.

What can be quickly found both in Billings and in his English
predecessors is a style that is consistently florid throughout a
melody. Although floridity occurs often enough in tunes with
duple metrical signatures, this is a style that lends itself particularly well to triple meter, especially ³₂. With an iambic text, the
succession of halves and wholes becomes monotonous. And so a
pair of halves will be substituted for the whole note or a pair of
quarters for the half. Almost any tune in Billings' NEPS will
provide a good example, such as *Union*. (Example 64) Here,

in bars four, seven, and eight, the substitute for the whole note
is dotted quarter, eighth, half. Often this dotted-note figure be-

comes the dominant feature of the tune, as in Billings' *Marble-head* (Example 65) or Williams' *Beconsfield*. (Billings' *Malden*

65. Tenor

is very similar.) This figure became a cliché of Tans'ur's style, as in the tune, *St. Martin's,* which is still to be found in our hymnals. (Example 66)

66. Soprano

Come, Ho — ly Spir - it, heav'n - ly Dove.

The general floridity can be increased to the point where it seems a caricature of itself, as in Billings' *Dorchester*, where almost every accented syllable has a short fiotura upon it. (Example 67) The change to duple meter after the first phrase

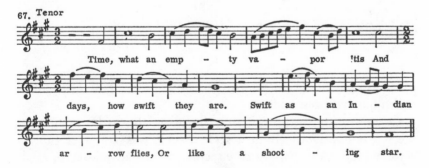

67. Tenor

Time, what an emp — ty va - por 'tis And

days, how swift they are. Swift as an In - dian

ar - row flies, Or like a shoot - ing star.

occurs in SMA; in the original version of the tune in NEPS the signature is erroneously kept as $\frac{3}{2}$ throughout.

The slightly florid patterns are usually not so stereotyped in duple meter as in triple, but often do become as elaborate as in Example 67. In duple meter also the floridity may become offen-

sive if applied in a stilted and mechanical manner, as in the tune
Knighton, found in Knapp. (Example 68) All the voices are

given for its first two phrases to show how rigidly the florid
technique has been laid on.

Of course, with the excessive floridity, the psalm composers
were attempting to attain a style which was really elegant, a
style which more sophisticated composers had mastered. This
style is evident in the five psalm tunes by Martin Madan which
were printed by Law. These are all for three voices, with the
melody in the soprano, and give the impression of being duets
for soprano and tenor, with instrumental accompaniment. They
are mostly of the hymn-anthem type, but *Leeds* illustrates the
style on a smaller scale. (Example 69) The general smoothness of

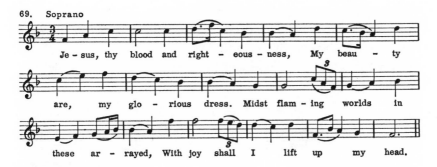

69. Soprano

Je - sus, thy blood and right - eous - ness, My beau - ty are, my glo - rious dress. Midst flam - ing worlds in these ar - rayed, With joy shall I lift up my head.

melodic progression differentiates these tunes from previous examples which we have shown, for the rhythmic motives are very much the same. Note particularly the appoggiaturas in bars four, eight, twelve, and fourteen—a token of Madan elegance.

Very seldom do the melodies of Billings' psalm tunes approach the Madan sophistication. Sometimes, however, a little of it breaks through the shackles of the four-voice harmonization. For example, in the latter half of *Petersburgh* the tenor has a lilt which is more common in Billings' anthems. (Example 70)

70. Tenor

But I de - scend to world be - low, On earth I have a man - sion too, The hum - ble spir - it and con - trite Is an a - bode of my de - light, Is an a - bode of my de - light.

From the examples already given, it is evident that some degree of floridity was the norm in the church music of Billings and his contemporaries. Usually the more extended melismas were reserved for important or descriptive words. The simplest type of melisma consisted of a group of even notes moving along a scale line, as the eighth notes in $\frac{2}{2}$ meter on the word "mighty" in Knapp's anthem, "I will sing unto the Lord." (Example 71)

migh   -   ty   wa - ters.

James Lyon, the first American church composer, shows similar treatment of sixteenth notes in $\frac{4}{4}$ meter on the word "trumpet" in his anthem, "Let the shrill trumpet's warlike voice." Oliver Holden, Billings' most important immediate successor, has just as clear an example of sixteenths on the word "sing," in his anthem, "Sing, O ye heavens." (Example 72) Similar instances

Sing

may be found in Billings, such as the melisma in eighth notes on the word "darkness," already shown in Example 23.

Extended passages in even notes are not at all common in the psalm tunes. At the end of the *Shoreham* tune, given by Adams, the tenor has twelve eighth notes in succession to the word "glory," and this is an extreme case. (Example 73) This tune,

Un - veiled in per-fect glo   -   ry   shows.

by the way, illustrates wrong metrical signature and barring: the first part of it is actually in $\frac{3}{4}$ meter, but is barred wrong; the part shown should be in $\frac{2}{4}$. In Lyon the tune is printed in C, which on the whole is a better key than A for the voices.

No lengthy passage in even notes was found in Billings' psalm tunes, but there is one which misses by the slightest possible margin. This is the fuguing tune *Milton*, in which the tenor sings sixteen notes to the first syllable of "constant," all except the first two being quarters. (Example 74) The florid tenor and

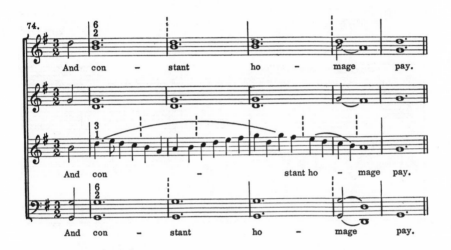

the sustained notes in the other voices, with their sonority increased by choosing notes, present a purely instrumental effect, rare in Billings or his contemporaries. Note that the tenor becomes duple with the word "homage." A careful examination of all the parts in this final phrase suggests that the real meter is $\frac{6}{2}$ for the accompanying voices and $\frac{3}{1}$ for the tenor, for a very interesting cross rhythm, similar to effects in our contemporary music.

There is a unique example of florid sixteenths with a signature of $\frac{2}{2}$ in the *136th Psalm Tune*, printed in Lyon. With a poetic meter of 66664444, the first four phrases are almost wholly in half notes; the next two introduce, responsively, shorter note values; and each of the final two, which are shown, begins with the sixteenth-note figure in two voices. (Example 75) The strik-

ing contrast between long notes and notes which are only one-eighth as long suggests nothing so much as the unexpected written-out ornaments in early Baroque keyboard music in England and Italy. The text printed with this example is that of the New Version Psalm 136; the Old Version is in the same meter. No text was given by Lyon.

At the opposite extreme from the sixteenth notes in Example 75 are the twenty-seven half notes by which Billings has represented "flying," from "The Lord descended," the same anthem from which Example 23 was taken. (Example 76) This appar-

76. Tenor

ently vigorous melisma would seem to demand a Presto tempo. Billings' Grave suggests hovering more than it does flying, and presupposes a greater lung capacity than amateur singers have! An already cited example from West (Example 26) shows on the word "works" a combination of eighth notes, triplet eighths, and sixteenths, for as neat an illustration of cross rhythms as one could desire.[10]

Daniel[11] has called our attention to a cliché of Tans'ur's melismas—the pattern of an eighth followed by two sixteenths, as in Example 77 on the word "King," taken from his anthem,

Psalm 47. He finds[12] a very similar treatment for the word "shake" in Billings' "I will love thee." (Example 78) Other

instances of this figure in Tans'ur can be seen in Examples 15, 18, and 28. Example 13 had contained the motive augmented, and Example 14 doubly augmented.

Very often a florid passage will be made up of several rhythmic patterns, as in the just mentioned Example 13, where Williams has set the word "O" with a dactylic pattern followed by even sixteenths. With Billings the departure from equality of note values may be for the purpose of including a tremolo, as on the word "laugh" in "Thou, O God." (Example 79) He has

[10] Daniel, *op. cit.*, p. 149 refers to a similarly complex passage in this anthem.

[11] *Ibid.*, p. 105.

[12] *Ibid.*, p. 205.

They shall laugh,

shall laugh   and   sing.

expressed the word "rejoice" in "Was not the day?" in much the same way, and that is logical enough. But he also used the same type of melisma for the word "forkèd" in "O praise the Lord of heaven," and this is an indication that his repertory of descriptive effects was somewhat limited!

Much more common than passages in even notes were those in dotted rhythm—perhaps the reflection of an almost universal performing practice for passages written in even notes. In Example 16 Williams' short melisma on the word "seek" was shown, using the rhythm of a dotted eighth and sixteenth. Lyon has similar, but more extended, melismas on the words "harps" and "organs," the latter being shown in Example 80.

With or   -   gans joined.

The *23rd Psalm Tune*, found in Lyon, is full of conventional short ornaments in dotted rhythm; then, in all the voices in the final phrase, there is a nineteen-note fiotura in dotted quarters and eighths. (Example 81) The $\frac{4}{4}$ signature here in place of $\frac{2}{2}$

My wants   are all sup-plied.

makes little sense, and one might remark that in general the tunes printed in Lyon do not differentiate as clearly between the two signatures as in most of the other collections.

Of course the dotted-note rhythm is often combined with

other motives, as in one of Arnold's elaborate tunes, *Shepshead*.
(Example 82) In a fuguing passage the tenor has a seventeen-note

melisma on the word "truth," in which the dotted rhythm is
smoothly combined with eighths. Again, in Knapp's *A Carol
for Christmas Day 1751*, a dotted eighth-sixteenth figure is ex-
pertly combined with even notes to form a twenty-one-note
fiotura, on the word "give."

A rhythmical motive which Billings liked, but which his predecessors did not use, consisted of a dotted eighth, sixteenth, and
two eighths. It might be called the Hallelujah motive, as it is the
diminution of the initial motive in Handel's *Hallelujah Chorus*.
In Billings' *Morning Hymn*, on the word "rolls," there is an
extended melisma in all the voices in which this four-note figure
is displayed prominently. (Example 83) A similar example

occurs in *Phoebus*, on the word "songs," and *West Sudbury* has
four repetitions of this figure in the tenor part, on the word
"pass."

Although a certain amount of floridity was present in the
other American collections examined, they contained no melismatic passages of the interest which exists in many of Billings'
tunes and in those of his English predecessors. One slight exception is the tune *Pennsylvania* in Shumway. (Example 84) Here,
at the end of a fuguing passage, all of the voices are florid on the
word "roll," with an extent of seventeen notes in the tenor part
and with good use of the Hallelujah motive just illustrated in

Billings. Because of the overlapping of phrases, the passage as shown begins *in medias res,* and all the voices are given so that the conspicuous parallel fifths become evident.

A most striking melisma occurs toward the end of the fuguing section of Billings' *Creation,* that most outstanding of all fuguing tunes, both in the beauty of its subject and the great skill with which it has been developed. Just before the final outburst, the tenor has a twenty-nine-note fiotura on the word "long," in which even quarters and the Hallelujah motive considered above are combined sequentially with happy results. (Example 85) In Billings' *Brunswick* there is a similar, but shorter, melisma in which all the voices join, on the word "pants." This tune is in F sharp minor, a key seldom used by Billings. Oddly enough, two tunes referred to above, *Phoebus* and *West Sudbury,* are also in this key.

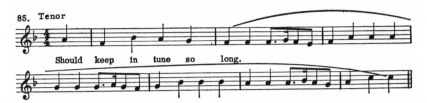

85. Tenor

Should keep in tune so long.

Billings' anthems also contain the Hallelujah motive; in "O praise God" it appears once on the word "trumpets," although the chief interest lies in the dotted-note melisma on "roll." (Example 86) In this passage Billings does not attain a very high

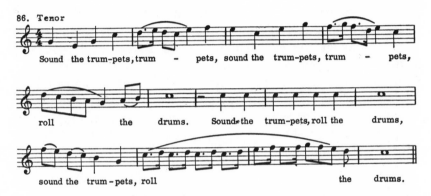

86. Tenor

Sound the trum-pets, trum — pets, sound the trum-pets, trum — pets,

roll the drums. Sound the trum-pets, roll the drums,

sound the trum-pets, roll the drums.

level of descriptive writing, although the contour of the melody at the beginning does reflect trumpet idioms. In the anthem "Sanctify a fast" the same figure occurs on the word "rejoice."

Again we find the Hallelujah motive on the word "chief," in a passage from "I charge you" that also illustrates changing meters. (Example 87) In this anthem the Scotch snap is exploited

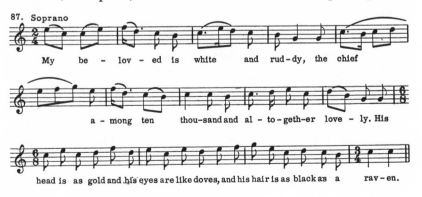

87. Soprano

My be - lov - ed is white and rud-dy, the chief

a - mong ten thou-sand and al - to-geth-er love - ly. His

head is as gold and his eyes are like doves, and his hair is as black as a rav - en.

charmingly, as on the words "belovèd" and "among" in the present example, and on "awake" and "love" in Example 88,

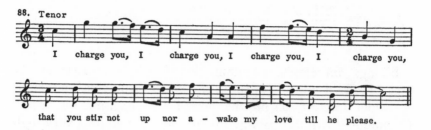

the latter representing the final variant of the rondo theme and featuring a smooth shift from triple to duple meter and a syncopated effect at the end reminiscent of Purcell and the 17th century. The snap may be found in Examples 10 and 33, from Shumway and Read respectively, while Billings' anticipation of "Ol' Man River" (Example 49) gives it in augmented form. An excellent precedent for the American exploitation of the Scotch snap is given by Daniel[13] from Tuckey's anthem, "Jehovah reigns." (Example 89)

We have already observed Williams' melisma on the word "O". (Example 13) In Selby's Thanksgiving Anthem, "O be joyful," the unimportant word "from" is stressed by a melisma in even notes. (Example 90) Exceptionally, Billings would also

introduce the melisma in a conventional way, with little regard for the importance of the word thus emphasized. For example, in a passage in "As the hart panteth" the important word is

[13] Daniel, *op. cit.*, p. 132f.

"remember," but "things" is extended by a melisma in quarter notes. (Example 91) The worst offense of this sort that he com-

mitted was on the word "whereof" in the anthem "When the Lord," and it may be forgiven because it occurs in a polyphonic passage where the tenor is less prominent than usual. (Example 92)

Worth noting as an exception among the psalm tunes of Billings is the fuguing tune, *Great Plain*, where the tenor has fourteen notes in dotted rhythm on the unimportant word "into." (Example 93) The definite duple rhythm implied here by

the sequential pattern in the tenor is confirmed by simultaneous accents in the other voices. Billings has said in a footnote: "Part of this tune is very badly barred, but I will leave it for the observation of the reader."

Even when the floridity is confined to a carefully chosen key word in the first stanza of a psalm tune, as is almost always true with Billings, the embellishment may fall on unimportant words in later stanzas. A happy exception is the tune *Shoreham* (Example 73), where the melisma occurs on "glory" in the fourth line of the stanza. In succeeding stanzas it would fall on "equal," "silver," "praise," "solemn," and then again on "praise." All of these words, with the possible exception of "equal," are worthy to bear the melismatic stress.

But consider Billings' *St. Enoch*. (Example 94) The text is

94. Tenor

Sing,   sing,   sing

Psalm 98 New Version, "Sing to the Lord a newmade song."
The tune begins with all of the voices intoning the word "sing."
Then, after a short rest, the tenor has two thirteen-note melismas
on "sing," strongly resembling the cantillation of a Jewish cantor
with their prevailing dotted rhythm. The accompanying voices,
not shown here, present a more complete text in stately, syllabic
fashion. Fuguing treatment later helps to make this an interesting, effective tune. In later stanzas the embellished words are
"The," "Of," "Let," "With," etc.—all of them unsuitable words
to be given elaborate melodic treatment. One might fervently
wish that, in a tune like this, as in many of the fuguing tunes,
only the single stanza would be sung.

It is impossible to sum up Billings' melodic style in a word, for
its variety is too great. We have seen that Billings, far more
than his English or American colleagues, has drawn freely upon
motives from folksong. But we have seen also how he has refined
these motives so as to present a melodic line that often reflects
a textual phrase to perfection. We have noted the moderate or
elegant floridity that was so prevalent in England in the 18th
century and which Americans found to their liking. But we
have noted also that only Billings among the Americans delighted
in the extended melismas for expressive purposes that are an
integral part of the melodic style of the operas of Lully, the
anthems of Purcell, or the oratorios of Handel. Such a style is
richly deserving of our praise.

Counterpoint and Harmony

Billings' texture in both the anthems and the psalm tunes is basically homophonic. The important thing to note, however, is that he invariably thinks of his vocal parts as strands of melody. To him, a passage is not in four-part block chords, it is in first-species counterpoint. Even in the bass part, where leaps of a fourth, fifth, or octave are common, these fit into a good, singable line. Billings liked to vary the texture by making the voices rhythmically independent, as in Example 92, near the end of the previous chapter. However, the complete absence of the suspension in Billings and his contemporaries is a curious negation of the pure polyphonic style.

At its strictest this rhythmic independence becomes "fuguing," which may be defined as the entry of voices in staggered fashion with free imitation. Daniel[14] has broadened this concept materially by listing three types of fuguing: imitative, non-imitative, and textual. I would rule out non-imitative entries, agreeing for the nonce with Macdougall, who says[15] that "in the 'fuguing tune' the voices must enter not only in sequence, but also on

[14] Daniel, *op. cit.*, p. 200.
[15] Macdougall, *op. cit.*, p. 55.

points of imitation." Textual polyphony (*Scheinpolyphonie*) occurs only incidentally. Daniel has shown an excellent example of it from Knapp's anthem, "Sing unto the Lord." (Example 95) One clear-cut example of textual polyphony from Billings should be sufficient. (Example 96) It is from the concluding section of

the Ordination Anthem, "O thou to whom all knees shall bow." The instrumentally conceived bass (unique in Billings' work) suggests the chiming of bells.

Twenty years ago, in his introduction to the Billings pieces edited by Clarence Dickinson and published by Mercury, Carleton Sprague Smith hailed Billings as the "creator of the unique fuguing tune." Lindstrom also called him the "originator," and Howard has a heading, "Billings, and his 'fuguing pieces.'" But even a casual look at 18th-century English tune-books, accessible in our major libraries, will show how absurd these statements are. Billings did not invent the fuguing tune, nor, despite his often quoted panegyric in *The Singing Master's Assistant* ("... the audience are most luxuriously entertained and exceedingly delighted"), was it of supreme importance in his own music.

The whole matter of the fuguing tune has been treated clearly and thoroughly in an admirable article by Irving Lowens.[16] The English origin of the fuguing tune is not a matter of debate. Its remote antecedents may be found in the motet settings of

[16] Irving Lowens, "The Origins of the American Fuging Tune," *Journal of the American Musicological Society*, Vol. 6, 1953, pp. 43-52.

psalm tunes during the Tudor period, and in the "tunes in reports" of the *Scottish Psalter*. Causton's version for the second tune for Psalm 139, first printed in 1563, may be cited as an example of a tudor motet setting. The text ("O Lord, thou hast me tried and known") is C.M. Dbl. There is some independence of voices in the first half of the setting, the counter tenor and then the bass being opposed rhythmically to the other three voices. At the beginning of the second half (Example 97), the soprano enters

alone and is imitated rather strictly by the alto in the lower fifth, by the tenor in the lower ninth, the bass in the lower fifteenth, and the alto in the lower octave. The remainder of the tune gets polyphonic treatment also, but without imitation. The entire setting is fresh and melodic in all of the voices, and is free from the parallels which few of the 18th-century psalm composers seemed to be able to avoid.

The above Causton setting has been printed in Maurice Frost's *English and Scottish Psalm and Hymn Tunes*, London, 1953. Frost has also printed three of the eight "tunes in reports" from the *Scottish Psalter* of 1635. A more interesting Scottish setting is that for Psalm 113, to the tune for this psalm that had appeared in the *Anglo-Genevan Psalter* of 1561, to William Kethe's text, "The children which do serve the Lord." The fine, long tune had originated in the *German Psalter* of 1526, and had been used for Psalm 36 in Calvin's *Psalter* of 1539. Example 98 shows the

setting of lines four and five, "Who from the rising of the sun Till it return where it begun." Throughout, the melody is in the tenor, imitated in the fourth phrase a bar earlier by the soprano and a bar later by the bass. The soprano also anticipates with syncopation the tenor entry in the fifth phrase. With the added interest of cross accents, this setting "in reports" of Psalm 113 is even more grateful to the singer and to the listener than Causton's setting of Psalm 139; in fact, it is completely captivating.

It would be instructive if a continuous history of polyphonic treatment of psalm tunes could be shown from the intricate imitation and rhythmic complexities of the "tunes in reports" to the fuguing choruses and the completely integrated fuguing tunes of more than a century later. The Puritan influence, however, broke off the direct development of the polyphonic style. After the Restoration, Purcell and a few of his successors resurrected much of the grandeur of the Tudor anthem. No doubt, something of the style of these sophisticated "cathedral" composers was imitated by the ill-trained "church" composers in their anthems and psalm tunes. Melodically, the 18th-century psalm tunes in general became more and more florid, and it is this floridity, together with the often crude and free imitation, that characterizes the earliest English examples of the fuguing tune.

The direct ancestor of the American fuguing tune appeared in the tune books of English psalm composers about 1760. Books which I have consulted include: John Arnold's *Leicestershire*

Harmony, 1759, with nineteen fuguing tunes; the tenth edition of Abraham Adams' *Psalmist's New Companion*, 177? (originally c. 1760), with fifteen; the fourth edition of William Knapp's *New Church Melody*, 1761 (1st ed., 1753), with ten; the third edition of the Tans'ur-Williams *American Harmony*, 1769 (1st Tans'ur ed., 1755), with seven.

Tans'ur has furnished a number of examples of the fuguing Chorus, in which the last two lines of a stanza are repeated with imitative entrances. Two of these have already been shown for their rhythmic irregularities. In Example 15 (p. 24) the voices enter regularly after four beats, in accordance with the actual meter. Only the bass begins on D, followed by three real answers on A. In Example 28 (p. 31) the bass answers the tenor after three beats; but the entry of the subject in both alto and then in soprano comes after five beats, the simultaneous accents in all of the voices giving rise to the actual $\frac{5}{4}$ meter for which this example had been presented. Example 15 is above average for Tans'ur's fugues; Example 28 shows him as his normal plodding self.

More common among the English psalm composers than the fuguing Chorus was the fugue as a part of the tune proper, as many as four fugues occurring in a single tune. Arnold prints the *Dishley* tune, which has a fugue at its very beginning and another at the end, the latter being shown in Example 99. The florid tone painting on the word "gladly" is representative of this English school. Although there is still some stiffness in the entries, the phrases overlap commendably in the various voices, unlike Tans'ur's fugues.

It is very difficult to find an English fuguing tune which is not disfigured by some grave flaw, such as the stilted phrasing of Examples 15 and 28. In Example 99 the harmony is in question, with two bare chords in bar six, parallel octaves and fifths in bar eight, and a free-for-all on the third beat of bar ten. The *Derby* tune found in Adams is one of the better English fuguing tunes. We saw in Example 5b how it rose above the limitations of wrong barring. And yet there are parallel fifths in the third and fourth bars of this example, as well as an Elizabethan clash in an earlier part of the tune. (Example 125)

Derby rates another sort of distinction also, for it is one of

Lord, for the liv-ing, for the liv-ing, for the liv-ing God.

shall I come and ap-pear be-fore God?

pear be - fore God?

teth for God for God.

many tunes in which the inevitable text repetition in the fuguing portion makes for ludicrous effects in later stanzas. Percy Scholes[17] has quoted two classical and possibly apocryphal instances of such repetition: *"He's our best bul-*wark still" and *"Bring down sal-*vation from the skies." (The parts in italics to be sung thrice.) In *Derby*, while the soprano is singing Example 5a, the bass has "In *trembling* and in fear"; in the following stanza this becomes "His *Son with-*out delay." In Example 5b the soprano sings, "See that with *rev'rence* ye rejoice"; in the next stanza, "Left in his *wrath ye* suddenly," and in the final stanza, "Then only *they that* trust in him." But perhaps we should not even smile tolerantly at the supposed foibles of our ancestors: as we lustily sing "Joy to the world" at each new Advent season, do not we also repeat strangely, "And won-, and wonders of his word"?

All of the English collections containing fuguing tunes that were mentioned in a previous paragraph were available in the American colonies before Billings issued the *New England Psalm Singer* in 1770. It contained three fuguing tunes, which are very much in the English manner. The fugue is attached as a Chorus; the entrances of the voices are a little mechanical in their regularity; the imitation is exact, in the octave and double octave; there is considerable floridity. All of these points except the floridity are illustrated by a fuguing passage in the anthem, "As the hart panteth," from this same collection. (Example 100)

[17] Percy A. Scholes, *The Oxford Companion to Music*, New York, 1938, p. 451

Here the music comes regularly to a stop five times in twenty bars, somewhat like the fugue in Mozart's *Musikalischer Spass* or like some of Tans'ur's fugues. In the "Dux" and elsewhere it is sometimes necessary to accent the second half note in the bar, which is not so strange, since the presence of quarter notes suggests $\frac{4}{4}$ rather than $\frac{2}{2}$. However, in the third bar from the end, Billings slips slightly from his usual standard by making the alto sing "áppear befóre God."

In Billings' later collections the imitation is often decidedly free, and the fuguing section is extended until it dominates the whole. Billings' second collection, the *Singing Master's Assistant*, contains ten fuguing tunes, of which *North Providence* is one of the best. (Example 101) Here the homophonic part lasts for only two phrases, with an imperfect cadence. With the usual repeat, the fuguing part is seven times as long, without a cadence until the end. The precise melody of the tenor lead on "Ten thousand" is heard again only in the tenor's second entry. Although the soprano entries are somewhat similar to the tenor's, the alto's and bass's are decidedly different. And yet all the voices are lavishly melodic, and are most cunningly placed in rhythmic opposition to one another. Here, as often, the prevailing iambic meter of the text is clothed with an exuberant bourée rhythm. This tune is a far cry from the stiffness of Example 100.

Lowens thinks that Billings' later fuguing tunes were influenced by what was to become a typical American style, although it too had its roots in English psalmody. His illustration 2[18] gives the facsimile of a page from Read's *Supplement to the American Singing Book*, on which Joseph Stephenson's *Thirty-Fourth Psalm* (c. 1755) and Louis Edson's *Lenox* (1782)

[18] Lowens, *op. cit.*, p. 50.

appear. The fuguing part is strikingly similar, bearing out Lowens' contention that Stephenson provided the model that was followed by the Americans. Lowens' example is not wholly characteristic of Stephenson's technique, since he frequently was much more elaborate than this, for instance in his *Third Psalm Tune*, which contains three fugues. The first fugue comes at the very beginning of the tune; the second and third have the same subject and dominate the longer second half of the tune. This latter subject has the typical rhythm shown by Lowens, but in a somewhat more interesting melodic form, which comes even closer to the initial bass entry in *Lenox*. Example 102 shows the third fugue in the *Third Psalm Tune*.

The rousing tune, *Lenox*, (Example 103) has had the most lasting fame of all the early fuguing tunes. As late as the seventh edition (Calvary Edition) of the Baptist *In Excelsis* in 1900,

Lenox had retained its fuguing texture, although of course the principal melody had long since been transferred to the soprano. There is fuguing also in the Presbyterian Church's *The Hymnal* of 1897. But, although the Methodist *New Hymn and Tune Book* of 1867 still retained the fuguing, the *Hymn and Tune Book* of the Methodist Episcopal Church, South, of 1889 printed the tune in completely homophonic style. In the latter form, *Lenox* is sung in countless churches today, usually to Charles Wesley's "Blow ye the trumpet."

The typical melodic formula in *Lenox*, with slight variations, is to be found in other tunes of Read's *American Singing Book*, which had eighteen fuguing tunes in all; in several of the nineteen fuguing tunes of Jocelyn's *Chorister's Companion* (1st ed., 1783; 2nd ed., 1788); and in a great number of the thirty-one

fuguing tunes in Shumway's *American Harmony*, 1793,—too many of the latter displaying Shumway's crude harmonic style.

The *Lenox* formula, however, is very hard to find in Billings' later collections. There is a good example in *Framingham* (Example 104), which is in A minor, like Stephenson's *Third Psalm Tune* (Example 102), and which has a very similar subject. Since it appeared in the *Psalm Singer's Amusement* in 1781, the year before *Lenox's* debut, it must have been influenced directly by Stephenson. (There are five fuguing tunes altogether in *Psalm Singer's Amusement.*) Two of the four fuguing tunes in the *Suffolk Harmony*, 1786, also follow the formula, and of these *Kittery* resembles Stephenson's *Third Psalm Tune*, even to key.

Billings' *Continental Harmony* appeared in print in 1794, later than the other American collections which were just mentioned. So, as Lowens surmizes, there is a bare possibility that some of the eleven fuguing tunes in this collection were influenced by American composers. Many of these tunes have the elaborate treatment already observed in Example 101, and often the freedom as well. If any feature of these tunes is similar to some of the fuguing tunes in American collections contemporary with them, it is in the length and complexity of the fuguing part. But this was a common characteristic of the Billings' fuguing tune before any of the other American collections had appeared.

In *Psalm 19*, one of the anthems in the *Continental Harmony*, there is a fuguing passage which well displays Billings' most mature style. (Example 105) Twenty-nine bars in length, it evades a cadence until the final bar. The subject is strong and striking, with a brief shift to eighth notes in the third bar which is recognizable whenever it occurs later. The entries of the soprano and tenor in the double octave and octave respectively are fairly exact in melody, and, although the alto entry is less exact and this part is somewhat less interesting, all four voices have almost complete uniformity in their rhythmic presentation of the subject. Parallel octaves are present and objectionable only in bar thirteen—the fifths in bars sixteen, nineteen and twenty are harmless and modal harmony is at a minimum. One awkward bit in the seventh bar could be eliminated if the bass were to sing quarters E and D on the word "in" instead of the half note

E. Especially pleasing is the redundant entry of the bass in bar eighteen.

Psalm 19 contains some interesting rhythmic clashes. Although the $\frac{4}{4}$ meter is valid at first, the half notes in the bass from bar six on denote an actual $\frac{2}{2}$ with implied shift of barline, confirmed by the soprano in bar eight, and by alto and tenor one bar later. Then, with the word "redeemer" in bar fourteen, the soprano opposes the other voices, and its accents are confirmed by the bass when this word recurs in the soprano in bar eighteen. The bass similarly opposes the other voices until bar twenty-two, after which the accents are uniform in all the voices. A careful choirmaster will bring out these clashing accents, which are just as valid in Billings as in the madrigals and anthems of the Tudor composers.

Billings' *Creation* is the best of all the 18th-century fuguing tunes. Lowens calls it a short anthem, but Billings himself designates it a psalm tune in his index. The only respect in which it differs from many another fuguing tune in double meter, that is, in an eight-line stanza, is that the third and fourth lines are reset with a change of musical meter from $\frac{3}{2}$ to $\frac{3}{4}$ after which the second half of the stanza begins much like the first half, thus giving an ABA′ form up to the fuguing part, where the meter changes to $\frac{4}{4}$. The fugual subject is reminiscent of *Country Gardens*, made popular by Percy Grainger. It enters ten times, with a certain amount of freedom, but with sufficient resemblance to the initial motive that it registers as the same. Toward the end, the tenor twice has a melisma on the word "long," the longer having been shown in Example 85. Since there is a modern edition of *Creation*, edited by Clarence Dickinson and published by Mercury Music Corporation, it will not be necessary to quote it *in extenso*. (It was a Gargantuan *faux pas* for Dickinson and C. S. Smith to couple this tune with a tiny canon and a full-scale anthem and then to label the combination "Three Fuguing Tunes"!) It will suffice to give the homophonic coda of *Creation*, which is of suitable dignity to round off this most exuberant of fuguing tunes. (Example 106)

106.

Strange that a harp of thou-sand strings, Should keep in time so long.

It cannot be emphasized too strongly that, although in beauty and finesse Billings' fuguing passages far excell those of his contemporaries, his fuguing tunes do not bulk large in his total output of psalm tunes. Lowens states that Billings composed thirty-six fuguing tunes, which would be less than 8% of the total tunes composed by him. He also found that of 286 American collections published between 1761 and 1810, about 90% contained some fuguing tunes, and that in the majority of these, about 25% of the total tunes were fuguing tunes. Thus the proportion of fuguing tunes in Billings is only one-third as great as in the average American publication in his generation and the generation following. This agrees with another statement by Lowens that at least four other American composers wrote more fuguing tunes than Billings did, and at least five composers had more lasting popularity for their tunes, as evidenced by republication in other collections.

Although Billings' harmony is strongly diatonic and triadic (Daniel found that only about 6% of his chords were sevenths), his penchant for melodious part-writing is responsible for combinations of notes that may be analyzed as more complex chords. The whole tribe of psalm composers in the 18th century eschewed even unprepared dominant sevenths; so that the seventh in the sixth bar of Example 26 from West is daring. A Billings seventh occurs in bar eleven of Example 44, and there is a passing seventh four bars later. Billings' common cadential formula, as in Example 44 or Example 19, often has the soprano moving in sixths with the tenor, and this might be called a passing subdominant seventh. It might more properly be so called when, as in Example 22, the bass moves from the third to the root of the subdominant chord simultaneously with the passing note in the tenor. Double accented neighboring notes, as in the third phrase of Billings' *Africa*, also give rise to a IV₇, followed by a vii°₇ in ⁶₅ position. (Example 107) The second bar of Example 40 also has a vii°₇

107.

which is approached and quitted by skip. In the fourth phrase of Billings' *Maryland*, there is a passing I₇, in ⁶₅ position. (Example 108)

108.

Melodic considerations are also largely responsible for the chromatic ninth chord after a dominant seventh which occurs in Billings' anthem, "And I saw." (Example 109) In the Amen

and root of Da – vid.

section of the anthem, "Blessed is he," there is a major ninth with appoggiatura function—perhaps an error in notation. (Example 110) The diminished triad was often found in root position, and

A – men, A – men, A – men.

the augmented triad was not completely unknown. Both occur in Example 111, together with a i₇ in ⁶₅ position; the source is Billings' tune *Hebron*.

The diminished seventh was practically non-existent. An instance in the tune *Wendover* in Adams must be ruled out as a typographical error, since it involves the leap of an augmented fifth in the bass. Billings' *Phoebus*, which contains the only bona fide diminished seventh observed, presents it so smoothly

that one wonders why this chord did not often occur spontane-
ously. (Example 112) Chromatic progressions were extremely

rare. The tune *Hatfield* (Example 113) contained the only

example found in Billings, and there was a similar progression
in Knapp's *The King's Anthem.*

Billings appeared not to be familiar with the augmented sixth,
although one can be found in Tans'ur's *Ryall.* (Example 114)

The Italian form of the augmented sixth chord is present in Lyon,
in the *Fifth Psalm Tune.* (Example 115) Other instances of the

Italian sixth occur in Tans'ur's anthem, "Blessed are they," in
French's "O sing unto the Lord," and in Wise's "Great is the
Lord."

The above examples of the dominant seventh and diminished seventh, and particularly those of the augmented triad and augmented sixth, arise through chromatic leading notes. Sometimes the demands of *musica ficta* resulted in a semitonal clash reminiscent of the practice of the Tudor composers. At its mildest, this is a license permitted in our own traditional harmony —the conflict between the two inflections of the leading note in a minor key. Example 116 shows the final phrase of Thomas

Weelkes's three-voice madrigal, "Cease sorrows now," in which the clash itself does not sound strange; but an 18th-century composer would more likely have treated the C and A as a double appoggiatura resolving on B flat and G while the C sharp was still sounding. In his tune *Vermont*, Billings *does* treat the clashing D and the B a tenth below it as appoggiaturas, resolving on the dominant ninth in E minor. (Example 117)

Near the beginning of Billings' anthem, "Was not the day?" there is a similar clash between D and D sharp, but in a major key. (Example 118) Here the alto makes a transition to the

dominant key, but leaves the impression of a chromatic neighboring tone. If the D's on "and" and "are" had been E's, the harmony would have been conventional. Note also that if the passage had been in A minor, with C's in the soprano in the third bar, we should not have considered it strange—an indication of how arbitrarily we judge such matters! These bitonal effects of Billings' in a major key are not common, but they can easily be found, like four-leaf clovers, by a little search.

But, even with the bitonality, the two examples given above, together with one in G minor in the tune *Weymouth*, represent the total of Billings' chromatic harmonic clashes. He was almost pedantically averse to a type of license in which his contemporaries indulged freely. Even without chromatic inflections, these other composers obtained piquant effects, just through ordinary contrapuntal means. Take, for example, the *Fifth Psalm Tune* presented by Lyon. Its fourth line is set in a fuguing style, with rather strict imitation. (Example 119) The clashing upper neigh-

119.

bors in the third bar are as simple as those in Example 107. On the third beat of this bar the bass C is an accented passing note. On the fourth beat, the A in the soprano seems to be an appoggiatura; but the definitely nonharmonic note is the B flat which follows it and which clashes of course with the A in the tenor. Later in the fourth bar, the soprano all but runs into the F sharp leading note. These are strong effects, but, set as they are in a G minor context, they are not felt to be really ugly.

G minor is also the key of the tune *Wendover* in Adams. In the third bar of the third phrase there is a particularly jarring instance of semitonal clash when both the bass and the alto logically sing F, while the soprano just as logically sings F sharp. (Example 120) The fact that the triad is incomplete intensifies

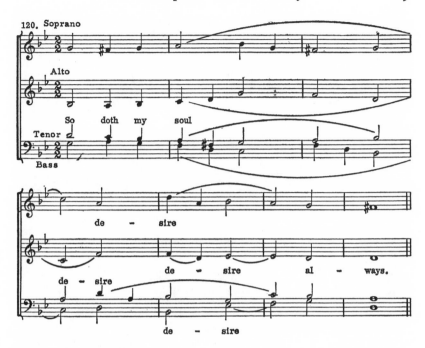

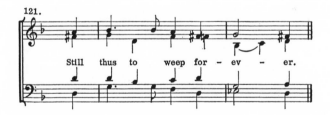

the dissonance. Example 121 contains the very same type of clash between F and F sharp as Example 120 does. And yet it is

from Thomas Morley's madrigal, "Since my tears and lamenting." Although the editor, Canon Edmund H. Fellowes, said that the sharp is "almost certainly an error," the kindred clash in *Wendover* confutes him.

A clash between a G and a G sharp is found in the sixth bar of the tune *Hoeton* in Arnold. (Example 122) The tenor proceeds correctly enough in A minor, but the alto wilfully goes her way in C major, the worst offense being the approach to G by skip from below and the continued rise from the G.

Had the quarter notes in the alto melisma (bass 6 and 7) been a third lower (an octave higher than the bass is a bar later), there would have been no difficulty. Note also the clash when the bass descends to C, while the tenor still sustains a B. (The beginning of bar 9.) Perhaps this could be called a retardation, but the annoying dissonance caused by it is typical of Arnold.

Except for the Billings illustration in Example 118, all of the examples of clashes shown so far have been in minor keys. In a major key the clash may be as pleasant and innocent as in the seventh bar of Example 28, where the lower-neighbor C sharp in the alto titillates with the upper-neighbor C in the bass. In the third bar of this passage, passing notes clash harmlessly.

Not all the semitonal clashes in major keys are as mild as that just mentioned. To understand these better, turn again to the Tudor madrigalists. Example 123 is from John Farmer's "Fair

nymph, I heard one telling." Two of its six voices have been omitted to clarify the progression. Here both the C and the C sharp are essential, and the contrary motion renders the effect delightful.

A post-Billings fuguing tune matches the Farmer example. The tune *Freetown* in Read has two fugues in its second half, both using the typical motive of *Lenox*. In the first of these fugues, the alto makes a short transition to G; but at the very instant that the F sharp appears in the alto, the bass has an F. (Example 124) This type of clash can be explained in Farmer,

not so much as the assertion of the claims of *musica ficta* in a general sense, as the ambivalent nature of the Mixolydian mode in the Tudor period, somewhere between a true Mixolydian and G major. Read must have been a belated Elizabethan, for his tune *Holland* has a similar clash. Even the first part of *Lenox*, as printed by Read,[19] has an F sharp clashing against an F, although no sharp appears in the original version.

In the first part of the tune *Derby* in Adams (a fugue in the second part which illustrates wrong barring is shown in Example 5), it is the soprano which makes the transition to the dominant key, while the tenor chooses to remain wholly in the tonic. (Example 125) The clash between the G sharp and the G is again in the Elizabethan tradition.

By "unjustified dissonance" Daniel refers to combinations of notes that cannot be explained contrapuntally as suspensions, anticipations, pedals, etc. How, for example, does one explain

[19] Lowens, *op. cit.*, p. 50.

the harshness in Arnold's *Loughborough*, where the soprano
sings three notes in succession (G, A, and B flat) that clash with
the tenor's G sharp? (Example 126) Is it an unusual augmented

sixth chord, with the first two soprano notes appoggiaturas? A D
in the alto would have strengthened this supposition. But the
clash is not too great, and there seems to be no feasible way of
softening it.

This sort of error is very rare in Billings. There is a passage
in his anthem, "Sanctify a fast," that is unpleasant, but that
almost defies correction. (Example 127) The bass is correct;

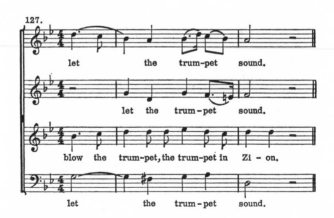

the tenor logically remains in G minor; the alto, while modulat-
ing to D minor, forms concords with the bass; the soprano line is
not wrong in itself—and yet the total effect is depressing. For

harmonic considerations one might wish to change the E flat
in the tenor to E and the C to C sharp, also making both F's in
the alto F sharps; but this does unwarranted violence to the
melodic lines. Fortunately, Billings does not confront us with
such a conundrum elsewhere.

Unjustified dissonance is not common among Billings' American contemporaries either. It is rather in the relatively untutored
English psalm composers of the preceding generation that it
sometimes cropped up. In Example 128a, from West, there are

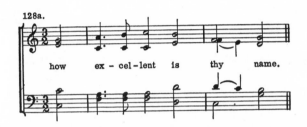

two strange chords. The tritone in the soprano is sufficient indication that West did not intend precisely these notes. Whether
the suggested emendation (Example 128a) is correct, it is difficult to say; at least it removes the difficulty.

We had seen in the third bar from the end of Example 99 from
Arnold's *Dishley* a combination of notes that defied analysis;
but each part is so melodic as it stands that one would hesitate
to tamper with it. The momentary absence of quintal harmony
in this example anticipates the strange harmonies often found
in the 19th-century shaped-note books. The tune *Holy Manna* in
Southern Harmony (Example 129) is a folk variant of the

familiar Rousseau tune *Greenville* ("Lord, dismiss us with thy blessing"), which can be sung with it as a discant. (Example 129a) Except for three F's in the soprano, all the voices are

pentatonic. One is tempted to change the first F to a G, the other two to D's, so that the soprano will not be an exception. Stark and arresting is the quartal harmony, spiced with bits of organum, as it is engendered by the pentatonicity. *Wondrous Love* in the same collection is a lovely folk melody which is greatly enhanced by an organum-like accompaniment. But there is nothing at all like these harmonies in the works of Billings and his confreres.

Toward the end of the fuguing section in *Wrotham*, from Adams, (Example 130) there is a passage that makes the hair

curl: in the second bar of the example the clash between the G sharp and G is understandable, but what about the third beat of this bar? The D sharp is an appoggiatura to the E; the tenor and the bass proceed smoothly to the octave C's; only the soprano causes trouble, for the F natural is not a proper lower neighbor in this context. If the soprano F is sharped, there is still a clash, but the progression makes more sense. (In the following bar the alto again has a D sharp which resolves on an E. But in no manner can the bass notes in this bar be explained logically— the dissonance cuts, and nothing so simple as adding an accidental will improve it.)

To conclude this collection of horrible examples, there is the beginning of Arnold's *Stanford*, (Example 131) which matches *Wrotham*. Not only is the tenor D sharp offensive against the unison F's in the soprano and alto, but this clash has been approached most unconvincingly, with augmented seconds in both the soprano and the tenor and with no clear harmony suggested by the movement of the bass. In the following bar the soprano has the raised leading note, G sharp, as it proceeds to A, while the bass stubbornly has G natural. The entire passage is extreme even for a slipshod composer like Arnold, who manages to

sound D sharp against another F natural before the welcome cadential chord.

If it appears that Billings has been slighted for several pages, with only three examples among the last eighteen, this has been to put him in the proper perspective. Throughout this book, Billings has been pitted against the field, as it were. In some respects he has been shown to be superior to the whole handful of his British and American colleagues; in others, quite similar to them. If he scarcely ever had F sharp clash against F, as many of the other composers did, this is an important element in his style. If he practically never wrote a baffling assemblage of notes, as the English composers sometimes did, he could not have been the ignoramus he has been often pictured.

In contrast to the clashes discussed above and also to the bare fifths so often present in the psalm tunes and anthems of the 18th century, are the duets in thirds that are sweet to the point of cloying. In a passage already cited from a Selby anthem (Example 90), the alto and the tenor sing as intimately as a couple of Italian gondoliers. Hans Gram, the Danish-American composer whose anthems are greatly admired by Daniel, has a section in his "Praise ye the Lord" in which the divided tenors sing wholly in thirds. (Example 132) Williams, in his anthem, "Arise, shine," has the soprano and alto singing in parallel sixths, which were not quite so common as the thirds. (Example 133)

Billings, in Example 38, has the tenor and bass sing in thirds. But he liked tenths about as well as thirds. In the first part of Example 44, the soprano and tenor parts run along almost wholly in tenths. Not infrequently he would commence a passage in tenths for one pair of voices and would then allot the response to another pair of voices in thirds, as in Example 134, from his

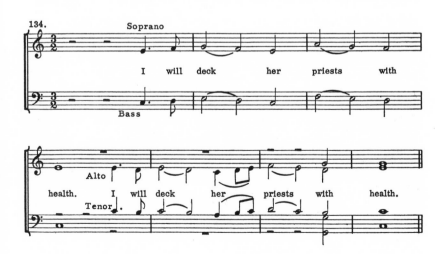

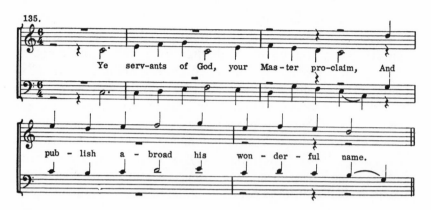

135.

Ye serv-ants of God, your Mas-ter pro-claim, And
pub - lish a - broad his won - der - ful name.

anthem, "O thou to whom." In Example 135, from his tune
Rochester, the alto and the bass sing largely in tenths, and the response by soprano and tenor is also in tenths. Occasionally a
passage in thirds for divided basses, as in Example 136 from the

136. Basses

Thou that hear - est the prayer, that
hear - est the prayer, that hear - est the prayer

anthem, "Thou, O God, are praised," goes so low as to grumble,
but these instances are few. One should refer also to the already
cited passage from "The Lord descended," (Example 24), in
which the triplet quarters in soprano and tenor run mostly in
sixths or tenths. Finally, the five parallel sixths between tenor and
bass to the words "very pleasant hast thou been," are one of the
most charming and expressive bits in "The beauty of Israel."
(Example 137)

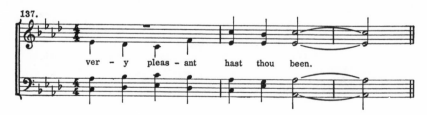

137.

ver - y pleas - ant hast thou been.

Parallel thirds and sixths are an expected concomitant of a style in which melody reigns supreme. It is the great tunefulness of all of Billings' voice parts that elevates him above the rest of the composers studied. This is even true of the waggish *Jargon*, of which the first two phrases are shown in Example 138. Of its

thirty chords, only the first is consonant; the others fairly bristle with seconds, sevenths, and ninths—pandiatonicism a century and a half before Slonimsky! And yet, except for some angularity in the tenor's second phrase, the parts remain wholly singable.

It was melody that was Billings' touchstone for the fuguing tune also. If his earliest specimens were little better than the Tans'ur model, it was probably because he had not yet learned how to write phrases that overlapped and, at the same time, melodic lines that were interesting. Significantly, it was the polyphony that had to yield. After he had developed a free fuguing technique in both his anthems and his psalm tunes, he was in a class by himself. And, although he sometimes experimented with it, he was never mesmerized by the tomtom beat of Edson's *Lenox*, as his younger contemporaries so completely were. To Billings, true melody could never be replaced by singsong rhythm, however boisterous its accents were.

Modality and Tonality

✖

The 18th-century psalm tunes reveal many traces of the ecclesiastical modes, more in the harmonization than in melody. It is to be expected that the presence of the modes should still be felt, since the heritage of 16th- and 17th-century psalmody contained many modal melodies. A quick check of the 164 Old Version psalm tunes proper in Frost's collection showed that 59 of them, or slightly more than one-third, were in modes other than the Ionian and Aeolian. There were ten Mixolydian tunes, thirty-five Dorian, and fourteen Phrygian. The Lydian tunes had long since become F major. In the course of time the Mixolydian tunes became G major and the Phrygian tunes C major. But some of the Dorian tunes continued to preserve the sharp sixth which is perpetuated today in the melodic form of the minor scale.

By modal harmony we mean an excessive use of secondary triads compared with classical harmony, especially the mediant; too great a use of chords in root position,[20] especially with roots moving by step in the major key, such as ii I, iii ii, and iii IV; in the minor key, the over-use of the lowered seventh degree, in v, III, and VII.

Most of the above characteristics of modal harmony necessarily follow from a desire to make the bass melodious. Billings' harmony is generally somewhat restless, the smoothly moving voices generating a rapid harmonic rhythm. As an exception let me mention a remarkable instance of static harmony, found twice in the anthem, "Who is this?" to illustrate the word "peace." The first time there are five bars of tonic harmony, and the second time nine and a half bars, with thirty-six consecutive melody notes belonging to the E major triad. Part of the second passage is shown in Example 139. (Any resemblance to the Prelude to

[20] Daniel, *op. cit.*, p. 195, found that 15% of Billings' chords were inversions in his early period; 20% to 25% later.

Rheingold is purely coincidental!) Here are crowded together some of the epithets applied to Christ, which are given complete in the discussion of this text on p. 12. Again, in Example 74 static harmony had been Billings' means of underscoring the word "constant."

Another striking descriptive touch occurs in Billings' "Thou, O God, art praised," where the text is "and the clouds shall drop fatness." Here Billings equals Chopin in static melody to suggest the patter of raindrops; of a total of sixty-seven notes in the alto part, there are sixty-four G's, two A's and one F sharp. In the short excerpt presented in Example 140, note the independence of the alto from the other three parts. One should refer also to the dirge-like tune, *Savannah* ("Ah! lovely appearance of death!"), in which the alto sings nothing but G's, twenty-four of them.

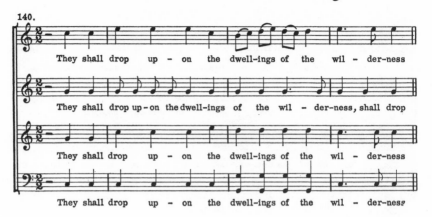

Modal harmony occurs at its starkest in Carpenter's tune
Hartford, the first half of which is shown in Example 141. It
contains no accidentals in its twenty-one bars. This, of course,
goes beyond the treatment of the Aeolian mode in the 16th
century, when the leading note would be raised in principal
cadences. Note the easy swing from i to III and back in bars
four and five, as well as the progression, i III v i, at the cadence,

bars nine to eleven. Note also the imperfect cadence in bars five and six—VII₆ v. (The first phrase of Arnold's *Loughborough* makes the imperfect cadence even more striking, with VII ii⁰ v. The fourth phrase of this tune is shown in Example 126.) The large number of incomplete triads (fourteen of thirty-two) and the parallel octaves (between bass and alto, tenor and soprano in bars seven and eight; between bass and soprano in bars eight to ten) are wholly characteristic of the style of composers showing modal tendencies. The smoothness of the tenor melody would make it a pleasing vehicle for L. M. Dbl.

Carpenter's *Hartford* does emphasize the tonic and dominant triads of D minor, and so is fairly clear in its tonality. But, frequently, in such hyper-modal tunes, there is such a delicate balance between major and minor that either of a pair of related notes might serve as tonic. Take, for example, the tune *Shepshead* found in Arnold, who had a gift, euphemistically speaking, for modal writing. This lengthy tune is in C major, without accidentals, and is almost entirely in ²⁄₂ meter. A short, complete passage in ³⁄₂ is given in Example 142. (The florid tenor part in

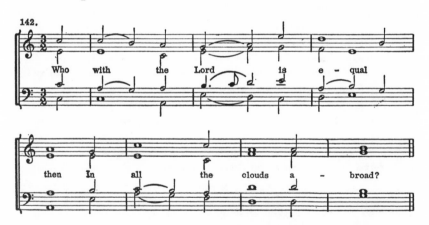

Example 82 comes immediately before this.) Note that, after the initial C triad, there is a great preponderance of the minor triads, ii, iii, and vi, and that in the imperfect cadence, ii V, impeccable though it is as a tonal progression, the voices are so arranged that II V would be preferred. Here, again, there are empty triads and parallel intervals—octaves between bass and soprano in bar

one; fifths between bass and alto in bar five and then between bass and soprano.

Some of Billings' younger contemporaries continued the modal style, thus bridging the gap to the folksy style so common in the shaped-note books, where modality was also very strong. A great many examples can be found in Shumway, as well as in Read. The tune *Naples* (Example 143) in the latter collection illustrates the extreme modality without accidentals, already exemplified in the two previous examples. There seems to be almost a textbook flavor of archaic progressions from the opening i III v through the VII₆ VI₆ v of the second cadence, to the III iv v i at the end of the fuguing section. The metrical signature for this tune is wrong: it should be $\frac{3}{2}$, with a single-note anacrusis. The fuguing section is as painfully stilted as could be imagined.

Although Billings sometimes used the tritest sort of harmonic progressions, with a preponderance of tonic and dominant chords, as in Examples 96 and 140, his style is often only too similar to that shown in the three examples just discussed. However, it should be pointed out that NEPS is almost completely devoid of accidentals, and that the extreme modality apparent in many psalm tunes and anthems in Billings' first collection is an illusion. A few sharps were added after the original engraving had been done; for example, two A sharps in the soprano of *Plymton*, a C sharp in the tenor of *Milton*, a G sharp in the tenor of *Pownall*, a C sharp in the tenor of *Lynn*. Sometimes it is possible to discover Billings' real intentions. The tune *Europe* modulates to the dominant in the first phrase; in the version printed in MM the needed natural is printed before the B flat. (Example 9) Similarly, the first tune in NEPS, *America* (unrelated to the tune for "God save the Queen"), modulates from D to A major in the first phrase, and the version in SMA contains the sharp for G.

Our first example of modality in Billings is from the anthem, "O God, thou hast been displeased." (Example 144) The final IV is explained by the fact that this comes at the end of a section, and the key of F follows; Billings never used the obsolete Lydian mode. The first four bars show a partial sequence in the tenor, and a modulation to the supertonic major, the latter being possibly unique in Billings' works. The consequent phrase provides the modal touch, with this harmony: V iii IV ii I V I IV, all

chords being in root position. (There is a suggestion here of the sturdiness of the well-known tune, *St. Anne*.) Note that the part-writing is impeccable, despite three stepwise progressions.

Example 145 shows the ending of Billings' early anthem, "The

Lord is King." Here, with harmony iii ii I V vi IV V I, there are four stepwise progressions. This time Billings has fallen into the trap, and two parallel octaves and as many fifths are the result. In a previously shown example from "Samuel the priest" (Example 22), overburdened with parallel fifths, the parallels are encouraged by the stepwise progression in the minor key: i VII VI v.

It is of course in minor keys that Billings might be expected to show the strongest modal tendencies. He never used the Phrygian mode, and even avoided the Phrygian cadence (ii III or iv V depending upon the mode) without which many of our familiar songs, such as "I've been working on the railroad," would lose part of their appeal to barbershop quartets. Example 150 contains an apparent exception. However, the V is not the cadential chord; the i in the following bar changes this to a conventional authentic cadence.

In general, Dorian remnants are so rare in the latter part of the 18th century that *Southwell*, with one Dorian sixth in the last phrase of the tenor part (Example 146), has a definitely archaic

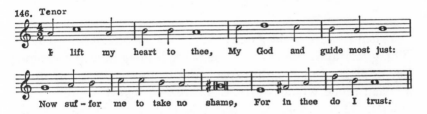

146. Tenor

I lift my heart to thee, My God and guide most just:

Now suf - fer me to take no shame, For in thee do I trust;

flavor, even for its own time. Although Billings never firmly embraced the Dorian mode, he sometimes flirted with it. A curious, but effective, use of the Dorian sixth occurs in "They that go down," where the strangeness of the B major triad in bars five and six is re-enforced by the sudden change to "piano," to picture the stillness of waves. (Example 147) The text of this

147.

Piano

so that the waves are still, are still, are still.

anthem lends itself readily to pictorial treatment, and it is possible to discover in it one example of the most obvious type of madrigalism, in the word "down." (Example 148) In the *Rose*

148.

in - to Heav'n and then down, down, down.

of Sharon, "rise up" is similarly treated, but with direction reversed. (Example 149)

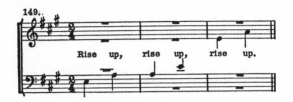

When we turn to the Aeolian mode, we are on less firm ground. Billings certainly does not use the raised leading note in the minor key as often as one might expect. But he uses it oftener than the Aeolian mode would warrant. There is a highly expressive refrain in "The beauty of Israel" that epitomizes in ten bars Billings' rather curious vacillation between minor key and Aeolian mode. (Example 150) Here the minor dominant occurs four

times, the major dominant only twice. It can be seen that both V and v are determined by melodic movement, E being used between two F's and E flat when it does not so lie. The one apparent exception is on the last beat of bar eight, where the E flat in the alto is needed to form an octave with the E flat in the soprano. Since there is no G in this chord, it might possibly be thought of as III instead of v.

Billings' anthems lend themselves much better than his psalm tunes to a thorough study of modal tendencies, since the former are in general of much greater length. The middle section of the anthem, *Psalm 44,* is in E minor, without modulations—unless the relative major be considered a modulation. In this minor section, the two forms of the dominant, v and V, occur with equal frequency, but the chord on the lowered seventh degree, VII, is much more frequent than that on the raised seventh, vii°. The tenor melody already shown in Example 37 suggests this ambiguity between mode and key. The major sections of this anthem also lend themselves to statistical study, since they lie completely in the key of E major save for four cadences in the dominant that need II and one in the relative minor needing III. Since there are about one hundred and eighty chords altogether in the two major sections (ignoring chords that are repeated immediately), the five foreign triads are statistically insignificant.

It is not difficult to show an accurate picture of Billings' progressions in *Psalm 44,* based on the total incidence of each chord and the most common chord movements. In both the major and minor sections, these typical progressions can be used to harmonize the first phrase of "Vom Himmel hoch," and it has amused me to do this, with tenor melody of course, a bit of floridity, and enough parallel fifths to impart the true Billings flavor. (Example 151)

Before leaving this question of modality in the minor key, let us turn to a much earlier Billings anthem, *Lamentation Over Boston*, which is entirely in the key of A minor. Its recurring harmonic progressions give the impression of a chaconne. If repeated chords are again regarded as a single chord, and also progressions of three chords that return to the first chord (such as i v i), the whole anthem can be reduced in a couple of stages (much as a topologist reduces a complex knot) to recurrences of nine four-chord formulas—the total of twenty-nine progressions includes five five-chord variants of the four-chord formulas. Here the formulas are arranged in order of frequency, with the number of appearances in parentheses: (a) i iv V i (7); (b) i v VI iv (5); (c) i VII III i (5); (d) v III VII i (3); (e) i III VII i (3); (f) i iv v i (2); (g) i VII v i (2); (h) i III v i (1); and (i) i v iv i (1).

Although most of the above formulas are cadential, only (a) and (h) belong to Schenker's set. Formula (a) occurs at the beginning of the anthem (Example 152); (b) at the beginning of

152.

By the riv-ers of Wa-ter-town we sat down and wept.

(i   v   i   v   i)   i   iv   V   i

the last phrase of the anthem; (c) incorporates the *Greensleeves* motive (*cf.* Example 53); (e) is in another early passage, following a tonic chord not shown (Example 153); one of the two

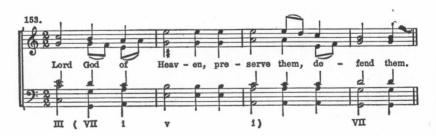

153.

Lord God of Heav - en, pre - serve them, de - fend them.

III (VII   i   v   i)   VII

occurrences of (f) was in Example 21 which comes five bars later than Example 153.

Unlike his impartial use of v and V in the minor portion of *Psalm 44*, Billings in his *Lamentation Over Boston* employs the minor form of the dominant thirty-six times to only ten times for the major form. Example 154 is a made-up chorale harmonization

which reflects the incidence of the progressions in this anthem, similar to Example 151 for *Psalm 44*. To those jaded moderns who have a passion for primitive harmony, these frequent minor dominants are a fascinating facet of Billings' style. But perhaps there were not quite so many of them as notated. Usually, Billings writes G sharp between two A's, as in Example 152. Now, in the second bar of Example 153 the G in the alto lies between two A's and, by the law of *musica ficta*, should also be G sharp. This is an improvement, since the phrase which begins and ends in C major now touches upon A minor instead of using a weak mediant. My made-up chorale, Example 154, also purposely contains such a *ficta* G sharp.

In my opinion, there is no question about the need for a G sharp at another cadence in the *Lamentation Over Boston*. This phrase (Example 21) has already been cited for its broadened cadence, and such a cadence is unthinkable without its leading note. In other Billings anthems, especially in NEPS, there are enough passages where accidentals are probably needed that a person who intends to perform a Billings composition must always be on his guard. More power, then, to the discriminating editor without a primitive stone axe to grind!

The large number of parallel fifths and octaves in Billings' music are as much a part of his general harmonic style as the modal progressions in which they often occur. It is this aspect of Billings' style that, among other things, has caused Lindstrom and Macdougall to call him "illiterate," and Howard to refer patronizingly to his "crude attempts." But parallel perfect intervals are no longer in the category of dirty fingernails; they, especially the fifths, are recognized as adding strength to the harmonic framework. And so some contemporary musicians would praise Billings for the very things for which the more tradition-minded writers have condemned him! The present writer, trained in the strictest of strict traditions, winces a little at some of the progressions; but, by and large, the parallels are convincing because of the general melodiousness of the parts involved.

But Billings was not the only composer of his age to perpetrate forbidden intervals. The example of textual polyphony from Knapp (Example 95) contains exposed parallel fifths. Read has an exposed pair of octaves in Example 20, and there are two fifths in the first part of his modal fuguing tune in Example 143. The parallels in Examples 141 and 142 have already been commented upon, in the modal tunes of Carpenter and Arnold respectively. In an example given by Daniel to illustrate a different point, Stephenson commits two sets of parallel fifths, two or three octaves, and a very harsh clash if all the parts are vocal. (Example 155) A flagrant case of parallels is shown by Daniel from an

155.

world with—out   end,   A   -   men

anthem by an American, Timothy Swan; it has the simplicity of strict organum. (Example 156) Church is almost free from for-

bidden parallels, and, despite other crudities, so is Tans'ur.
Arnold, with his fondness for modal progressions, has tunes that
are practically crawling with parallels, and there are a vast number in the collections of Law and Lyon. Babcock, Williams,
Adams, and Selby can also be counted among the violators. Of
collections by Billings' American contemporaries, Shumway and
Holden contain fully as many parallels as one finds in Billings.

One progression which occurs often enough in Billings' music
to be considered an earmark of his style, is I₆ vii₆ I. (In Example
159 the first tonic chord is in root position.) This is the 14th-
century cadence with double leading note, the Machaut cadence.
Examples 157 and 158 show the prototype,—final cadences of

Machaut motets in the Mixolydian and Dorian modes. Of eight
examples of this progression noted in Billings' psalm tunes, only
three are in cadences, where the stark, modal effect would be
most pronounced. The most archaic example is in the tune
Beneficence, which is L.M. Dbl. With the second half of the
tune the meter changes from $\frac{4}{4}$ to $\frac{6}{4}$, and at the beginning of this

fifth phrase, the progression I vii₆ I occurs, the parallel fifths giving an effect almost of organum. (Example 159)

Another example of the non-cadential Machaut cadence is found in the second phrase of *Majesty*, where the progression takes its more familiar form, with the first tonic chord inverted. (Example 160) Another good example is to be found in *Brattle*

Street, and others occur in fuguing tunes, such as *Egypt* and *Gilead*, which are difficult to illustrate briefly, because of overlapping phrases.

A clear and excellent example of the Machaut cadence is in the second phrase of the carol, *Judea* (Example 161). Clarence Dickinson for Mercury has changed the final note of the bass in this cadence from F to C, and so, by a strange coincidence, has

Walter Ehret for Lawson-Gould. This arbitrary alteration not only completely ruins Billings' harmonic progression, but also spoils the bass line, which is an imitation of the tenor melody in the first phrase.

The only example of the Machaut cadence found in a minor key was in the second phrase of *Hebron*. Here, since the leading note of the key was not inflected, the raised fourth degree resulted in the augmented triad for which this passage has been cited. (Example 111) The entire tune would sound better in the major key, without any alteration except in key signature, and one surmises that Billings may have originally conceived it in major. The Machaut progression is almost completely absent from church music by composers other than Billings. A notable exception is the tune *Cranly*, found in Adams. At the point shown, at the end of the third phrase, the music modulates from A to E, with the tenor taking a second leading note. (Example 162) The

clash between the A sharp in the tenor and the A in the soprano adds to the archaic impression.

The third phrase of the tune *Winter* in Read also has a Machaut cadence (Example 163); the root position for the first tonic chord makes the progression similar to that in Example 159. A passage in French's anthem, "O sing unto the Lord," has a

variant Machaut cadence, iii vii₆ I, although the alto, by her B flat, tries to make this a more conventional cadence. (Example 164) This combination of harmonic techniques of the 14th and

17th centuries has a fearfully fascinating effect. The three examples just discussed are the only ones I was able to find in composers other than Billings.

The progression I₆ II I, with the first tonic chord always in the ⁶₃ position, is similar to the Machaut cadence, both in its rarity and in its evocation of a remote musical past. It resembles the Landini cadence, which had the melodic progression, 7 6 8, as in Example 165,[21] the final cadence of Landini's ballata, "Chi piu

le vuol sapere." Only one of seven instances noted in Billings' psalm tunes (four of them are in SMA) used the progression in a non-cadential manner. This was the tune *Bethlehem*, to the familiar words, "While shepherds watched . . ." This is treated as C.M. Dbl., the second half being fuguing, with a change of metrical signature. In the homophonic final phrase the word "glory" gets florid treatment, and it is here, on the word "and" between two cries of "glory," that the II occurs. (Example 166) (A similar progression occurs near the beginning of the anthem, "The states, O Lord.")

[21] Parrish and Ohl, *Masterpieces of Music Before 1750*, (New York: W. W. Norton Co., Inc.).

The simplest possible presentation of the above progression, cadentially used, is in the second phrase of the tune *New North,* one of the few tunes in Billings which are completely syllabic. (A pair of quarter notes in the alto in the third phrase mar what would otherwise be a completely white page of half and whole notes.) The solemnity conveyed by the simple rhythm and the strange cadence is enhanced by a couple of pairs of parallel fifths. (Example 167)

An example of this cadence in triple meter is in the second phrase of *Philadelphia* (Example 168), where the passing note

in the soprano is a usual concomitant of the progression, thus making it I₆ II (vii₆) I. In Example 92, from the anthem "When the Lord," the roles of the soprano and tenor are reversed and the movement in the alto part lessens the cadential effect. Other examples of the I₆ II I progression are found in cadences—but never in a final cadence—of *America, Rocky Nook*, and *Moriah*. (One should add that Billings had a predilection for using this cadence in the key of D.) No examples whatever of the above progression were located in composers other than Billings.

If the Machaut cadence and the related quasi-Landini cadence are genuine touchstones of Billings' style, we have also noted that he was by no means alone in perpetrating modal harmony and with it those pesky parallel fifths and octaves. But, oldfashioned and austere as this harmony sometimes seems when played, it assumes its proper, subordinate place when the music is sung. Billings, the melodist *par excellence*, does not disturb us with his over-generous mediant triads in root position, since the mediant repeatedly graces the melodic line of the bass. So long as the ancient pentatonic motive, A G E (no pun intended), retains its melodic validity, just so long will it be a task of supererogation to insist upon every G being sharped in a Billings tune in A minor. On the other hand, if a single leading note is supposed to be good, perhaps two leading notes will be better, even if one must invoke the shades of Machaut and Landini to gain authority for their use.

Texture and Form. Conclusion

The hymns in our modern hymnals usually appear in such staid four-voice settings that we are inclined to forget that our ancestors may have sung these same hymns with a more interesting and varied texture. Take, for example, the choosing note. This was an extra note in a voice, so that the singer was free to choose which note to sing. Thus choosing notes were not quite like the *divisi* of a string player, where both notes are given equal stress, although in practice this is what probably happened. The choosing note might appear in a cadence, to fill out an incomplete chord, as in Tans'ur's *Dunchurch*, where the alto is given both the third and the fifth of the triad. (Example 169) In such a case

the choice might have been difficult to make, for, whereas today we should unhesitatingly choose the third, more cadences in the 18th century contained the bare fifth. In a very similar cadence in Tans'ur's *Chesterton*, the soprano has both root and third. (Example 170) The choosing note might also occur as a bass

octave, for greater sonority in a cadence in G or F, as in *Derby*, found in Lyon. (Example 171) This is a use for the choosing

note that is still found in our hymnals, as in the final cadence of
the tune *Hamburg* ("When I survey the wondrous cross").
(Example 172)

Billings was fond of the choosing note, frequently doubling a
part for a note or two or even for most of the tune. Sometimes
he would have bass octaves almost entirely, as in *Lancaster*, where
there are twenty-eight octaves and only four single notes in the
bass, as well as seven choosing notes in the alto. The first phrase
is given in Example 173. In this tune, as in the vast majority of

tunes in NEPS, there are no accidentals. A G sharp in the soprano
at the end of the phrase would be an improvement.

In NEPS, Billings' love for choosing notes really carried him
away from a reasonable situation for a normal choir. Not infrequently he would have many "triple stops" in a part, as in
New Boston, where the soprano has seventeen triplets, as well as
nine doublets, but only fourteen single notes. With four exceptions the bass is in octaves. The tenor, of course, is not divided,

and in this tune the alto does not happen to be divided either.
(Example 174 shows the fourth phrase.) The smooth melody

is very much in the tradition of the solemn older type of psalm
tune, but the part-writing leaves much to be desired in melodic
interest. The alto is especially monotonous, with thirty-two A's
out of forty total notes.

The tenor in the above tune has three high A's, this being the
upper limit in Billings, although a B flat can be found in the
anthem, "Hear, hear, O heav'n," and even a soaring B natural in
"The states, O Lord." (Example 175) If this peak seems very

high, one might assume a somewhat lower pitch level than we
have today. What, then, of the low D's that occur so frequently
in bass octaves? These surely needed instrumental performance.
But why then did Billings not write low C's more often in the
bass? I cannot answer this question. Exceptionally there are
C's in Examples 29 and 145, and also in the tune *Chesterfield*,
which is further distinguished by sixteen "triple stops" in the
alto and twenty-one octave D's in the bass, the dull harmony con-
sisting mostly of the tonic chord. The first two phrases of
Chesterfield are given in Example 176.

The ultimate in subdividing a part occurs in *Hanover*, where the second phrase (Example 177) has three bass "quadruple

stops." With choosing notes in the soprano also, two of these chords contain eight notes, achieving a remarkably sonorous effect. There is a quadruple stop in the soprano in the tune *Dickinson.*

Unfortunately, the bass choosing notes were not always octaves, and then there was the possibility of roughness arising from low sixths or thirds. (The only fifths found in the bass were those present in two of the quadruple stops in *Hanover*, discussed above.) There is the further possibility of an inferior harmonic progression engendered by the different position of the chords. It is a sound rule, although not without exceptions, to say that, where the intervals are not octaves, the upper choosing notes in the bass will produce a stronger effect than the lower.

Frequently, of course, a $\frac{6}{4}$ chord results from the addition of a sixth or fourth below the original bass. Sometimes the $\frac{6}{4}$ will occur like a pedal, with only slight loss of harmonic strength, as in the third phrase of *East Town.* (Example 178) Here there is a bass

sixth in the first of the $\frac{6}{4}$ chords and a fourth in the second, the latter being somewhat less pleasant. Again, an unaccented $\frac{6}{4}$, with static bass, may suggest a passing chord, as in the second phrase of *New Hingham*, where the upper bass line, moving by step to E, tends to counteract the leap to the E in the soprano. (Example 179) Note that the bass third in the previous chord, as well as the fourth, sound rough in this low register.

In the third phrase of *Wellfleet* (Example 180), the first A in the bass is rather like an appoggiatura, and the accented $\frac{6}{4}$ is tolerable, although it would have been better if the A and G in the

bass had not been doubled two octaves higher in the alto. Much weaker is the $\frac{6}{4}$ which is approached with static bass and quitted by leap, as in the fifth phrase of *Cambridge*. (Example 181) Here

the two low sixths, as well as the low fourth, give a grumbly impression. In his almost universal lack of accidentals in NEPS, Billings has failed to supply a necessary sharp to the F in the alto.

And so, although the choosing notes often made for somewhat less pleasing chords and inferior progressions, they were not too much of a hindrance on the whole. The great wonder is that Billings should have contemplated so large a force of singers and players that the divisions could be made satisfactorily. He probably discovered himself that his maiden efforts in creating added sonority were not very practical, for in his later collections the choosing notes are used with discretion and never in excess. (There are choosing notes in about a score of other examples in this book.)

Another common means of obtaining variety of texture in Billings' day, both in psalm tunes and in anthems, was the responsive or antiphonal treatment. We are accustomed to having anthems broken up by solos or duets. But it is a rare exception in a hymn tune when soprano and alto are answered by tenor and bass, as in Handel's *Antioch* ("Joy to the world"), to the words, "And heaven and nature sing." Just as rare is the texture in another favorite Christmas hymn, *Adeste Fideles*, where the refrain, "O come, let us adore him," is begun by soprano alone, while the bass does not enter until the third phrase.

Although the responsive style probably had its roots in the verse anthems (those with sections for one or more solo voices) of the "cathedral" composers, the earliest British collection examined in the present study, John Church's *An Introduction to Psalmody*, had neither fuguing nor responsive tunes; Tans'ur and Lyon had somewhat fewer fuguing than responsive tunes; Adams, Knapp, and Law preferred the fuguing type by a small margin, and Arnold had twice as many fuguing as responsive tunes, often having fuguing sections in the latter also. Billings was in a class with Adams, Knapp, and Law, with two-thirds as many responsive as fuguing tunes. He very seldom combined the two techniques in the same tune. Billings' American contemporaries ran heavily to the fuguing tune, with a 2:1 ratio in Jocelyn, and more than 3:1 in Holden's *Laus Deo* and Read. Of the new tunes printed in Shumway's collection, thirty-one had fuguing treatment and only one was responsive.

The simplest type of respond has the four-voice texture throughout except for a short solo. For example, in Billings' *Savannah*, the third phrase is a bass solo. (Example 182) A simi-

lar bass solo, with choosing-note octaves, forms the fifth phrase of the C.M. Dbl. tune, *Majesty*, of which the second phrase was shown in Example 160. Read has a respond near the end of the tune *Pembrook*, which, in S.M. Triple, is really a hymn anthem. In the coda the soprano briefly appears alone, answered by the tutti. (Example 183) Another example in Billings is *Sudbury*

(erroneously called *West Sudbury*), in which the fifth phrase of a Double Meter tune is allotted to the bass, with an obbligato divisi part in thirds. (Example 184)

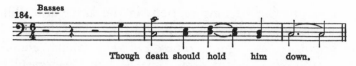

Though death should hold   him   down.

A short duet also provides pleasing variety of texture. In Oliver Holden's famous tune, *Coronation* ("All hail the power . . ."), the fifth phrase was originally a duet for soprano and bass (Example 185), and is somewhat unmanageable in its present-

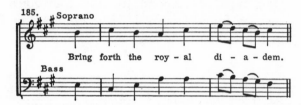

Bring forth the   roy - al   di - a - dem.

day four-voice setting. Billings' *Cobham* has a similar duet for soprano and tenor and his *Invocation* for alto and bass. A trio occurs in the seventh phrase of *Old North*, where only the tenor is silent, taking breath, perhaps, for the final phrase. Jocelyn gives two C.M. tunes on successive pages in which a duet briefly breaks the four-voice texture; in fact, in *Psalm 20* the break for tenor and bass is for four syllables only. (Example 186)

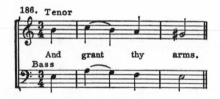

And   grant   thy   arms.

A tune may begin with a duet, as in the C.M. *9th Psalm* printed in Lyon, which has two phrases in $\frac{4}{4}$ meter for soprano and bass, changing to four voices and a $\frac{3}{2}$ meter for the remaining three phrases. The duet is given in Example 187. The L.M. tune *Dagen-*

ham in Lyon has an even more extensive solo portion of four phrases for soprano and bass, followed by a two-phrase tutti Chorus.

From a single initial duet to two duets is but a short step, taken by Billings in his tune *Rochester*, already shown in Example 135 to illustrate parallel tenths. Adams prints a tune with similar treatment; in *Wendover*, soprano and tenor are answered by alto and bass, after which the tutti takes over, and there is a fuguing section at the end. The *New 113th Psalm Tune* in Lyon has a phrase for tenor and bass, which is then repeated verbatim; the next phrase is for soprano and bass, after which the tutti assumes charge, again with the literal repetition of a phrase.

The paired duets may also occur in the middle of a tune, as in two tunes in Lyon, the *136th Psalm Tune* and the *Fourth Psalm Tune*, in both of which the contrast is provided by a duet for soprano and tenor answered by alto and bass. In *Laus Deo* the Ascension Day hymn, "Hail the day . . ." is set to Bull's *Middleton*, in which the third phrase is assigned to soprano and alto, answered in the fourth phrase by tenor and bass. The passage is worth quoting, as its verve reminds one of Billings. (Example 188)

188.

Christ a - while to mor - tals giv'n.

Re - as - cends his na - tive heav'n.

Beyond these simplest forms, there are many different possibilities for varying the texture of a psalm tune, only a few of which will be mentioned. Adams is very fond of giving fairly elaborate solos to all four voices in turn, after which the third and fourth lines of text are repeated by the tutti as a Chorus, although, unlike some of the other psalm composers, Adams does not use this word. Examples are *Leatherhead* and *Barrah*, with solos by bass, tenor, alto, and soprano, and *Banstead* and *Orpington*, both with solos by tenor, bass, soprano, and alto. In each of these groupings of voices the order of entry is like that of the exposition of a Bach-type fugue, although these are not strongly imitative responses.

A fifth example of Adams' practice of quadruple solos is *Hadlow*, where still another favorite fugal order of voices is observed—alto, tenor, bass, soprano. Here the tutti part, to the last two lines of a six-line stanza, comes to a cadence, after which the bass is heard alone for a bar and is answered by the alto an octave higher. Then, following a tentative bar, the entire tutti part is repeated. The stuttering effect of the "Ci-, ci-, cities . . ." is so reminiscent of the "K- k- k- Katie" of First World War fame that a few bars of the music are given, beginning with the respond. (Example 189)

The tune *Darking* in Lyon also begins with four solos, using the second Adams order (tenor, bass, soprano, alto), after which the Chorus has a tutti phrase followed by fuguing. To save space, Lyon has printed the four solos one above the other, which gives a somewhat bizarre harmonic impression to one taking a quick look at it. The fifth phrase, for tutti, allots the same melody to the tenor which the solo soprano had in the third phrase, and this gains added unity for the tune.

A somewhat similar pattern is to have several solos, each accompanied by the bass. An instance has appeared in Example 6, which shows the first part of Billings' L.M. Triple tune, *Stockbridge*. Here the first phrase is given to the bass alone, the next to tenor and bass, the third to alto and bass, and the fourth to soprano and bass, followed by the usual Chorus. Other Billings tunes, with the precise order of entries as in *Stockbridge*, are *Smithfield* and *Haverill*. Billings' bass in these three tunes is of proper duet type, running in parallel thirds and tenths with the melody. Tans'ur's *Chesterton* also has the pattern of these Billings tunes, and is unified by phrase repetition, as in Lyon's *Darking*, for the Chorus concludes with the tenor singing the melody of the soprano solo, the bass part being identical in both phrases.

In the second and third phrases of *Chesterton* the bass has no melodic function, merely giving harmonic support to the solo voice. It seems highly probable that in this Tans'ur tune, as well as in other tunes in which the bass seems to tag along unnecessarily, an instrumental performance was indicated. (Example 31, from a Tans'ur anthem, was an extreme case, for the continuo was not in the same rhythm as the melody and so a vocal performance was not to be considered.) Although the lowest choosing bass notes in Billings' music must have been for instruments, I am not so sure about these bass accompaniments to solo voices. In Example 6 the accompanying bass was vocal; but elsewhere, as in his anthem, "The Lord is ris'n indeed," the bass seems sometimes to be filling a harmonic function inconsistent with Billings' usual tunefulness. As I have said in connection with Billings' modality, the conductor will have to exercise his best musical judgment as to the performance of such puzzling passages.

Another common pattern is to alternate the tuttis with duets, to obtain a sort of five-element textural rondo. In Billings' *Philanthropy* the first tutti is followed by a duet for soprano and tenor; then comes another tutti, followed by a duet for alto and bass; a final tutti rounds the tune off. In his *Bellingham* the first four phrases are for the tutti; then, with a change of meter, the bass begins a phrase alone, but is quickly joined by the tutti; then the soprano and bass, largely in tenths, sing a phrase, after which the tutti has three more phrases to finish. Lyon's *33rd Psalm Tune* has a pattern similar to *Bellingham:* to a lengthy tutti is adjoined a duet for soprano and alto, to which the tutti responds briefly; then a suavely florid duet for tenor and bass is continued by the tutti to end the tune.

One of the most elaborate textural patterns is in Billings' Christmas hymn, *Emanuel,* with eight elements: ATB, SA, Tutti, TB, ATB, STB, ATB, Tutti. Except for the second element, the tenor participates in each of these combinations and has the principal melody, as was seen in Example 58. *Burlington,* to a Relly text, has nine elements: TB, Tutti, SB, ATB, Tutti, SAB, ATB, SB, Tutti. *Hartford,* also to a Relly text, has ten: SAT, STB, Tutti, AT, Tutti, S, ATB, Tutti, AT, Tutti. As none of these Billings tunes is inordinately long, the texture keeps changing every few bars.

Arnold's *Thrussington* (excerpts from it are in Examples 3 and 4) is comparable to the above Billings examples but is more interesting, formally speaking, for it includes five tuttis, alternating with pairs of voices, for a nine-part textural rondo: Tutti, SA, Tutti, AB, Tutti, TB, Tutti, AB, Tutti. This setting is sufficiently long that there is more variation in the length of the elements than in the Billings tunes, and this helps the architecture.

What gives added interest to some of the Arnold tunes is the combination of responsive and fuguing treatments. Billings, it will be remembered, practically never combined the two techniques in the same tune. Mention has already been made of psalm tunes in the collections by Adams (*Wendover*) and Lyon (*Darking*) in which a fuguing section formed the climax of a tune with varied texture. Tans'ur has two responsive tunes also (*Westerham* and *Upminster*) in which there is a fuguing section in the final Chorus. Two Arnold tunes afford somewhat greater variety than those just mentioned, both of them containing eight elements: *Leicester* has a Tutti, then AB, Tutti, Fugue, Tutti, SB, AT, Tutti; *Hathorne* has Tutti, Fugue, Tutti, AT, S, Tutti, Fugue, Tutti. The musical content of these Arnold tunes is low, but their architecture is excellent.

The amazing thing about the more elaborate responsive psalm

tunes, with or without fuguing, is that this great variety of texture was accomplished within the rigid framework of a poetic stanza, or at most of a double or triple stanza. In the anthems there was usually the much greater freedom afforded by a prose text, and Billings' cunningly chosen anthem texts offered limitless possibilities. So it may be taken for granted that greater variety of texture exists in Billings' anthems than in his psalm tunes. For example, "Hear, hear, O heavens," an anthem for Fast Day, has twenty-five textural elements: Tutti, TB, Tutti, B, T, S, Tutti, S, Tutti, etc. It would seem to need some unifying device if it prove not to be utterly chaotic. Billings, in fact, has provided three such devices. In the first place, after the first seventeen textural elements, the meter changes from $\frac{2}{2}$ to $\frac{3}{4}$; then, after seven more, there is a tutti coda in $\frac{4}{4}$

Furthermore, the last two elements outlined above, soprano answered by tutti, constitute a four-bar refrain (Example 190)

190. Soprano

ah,   sin - ful   na - tion,   ah,   sin - ful   na - tion.

which returns twice, its final appearance being immediately before the change to triple meter. Additional unity is secured for the first and longest section by a four-fold modulation from F minor to E flat major and back again, each time with different text and slightly varied melody. (The first modulation, the second tutti in the outline, is shown in Example 191.) Both the $\frac{3}{4}$ section and the coda modulate to E flat also, but without the melodic similarities noted in the first four modulations.

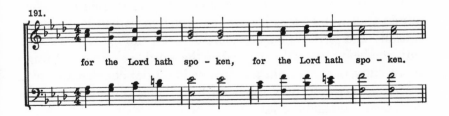

191.

for   the   Lord hath   spo - ken,   for   the   Lord hath   spo - ken.

The refrain in Example 190 is much shorter than Billings' norm, which is eight or ten bars, as in "I charge you, O ye daughters of Jerusalem," one of the most charming of Billings' anthems. Its rondo refrain occurs four times and has been chosen in Example 88 as a specimen of Billings' more ornate melody. The first occurrence of the refrain melody is as a soprano solo, which is then repeated by the chorus. The "couplets" are all for solo voices: soprano and tenor; tenor and soprano; soprano.

A similar alternation of solo voices with choral refrain is found in the Funeral Anthem, "Samuel the Priest," where the three later appearances of the refrain ("Have pity on me, O ye my friends") are indicated simply as a Dal Segno—"See Chorus." This anthem concludes with a short coda, the latter part of which has been selected to illustrate cadential broadening in Example 22. In "I will love thee," the returning refrain is also heralded by "See Chorus." The triple meter of this Chorus contrasts pleasingly with the $\frac{2}{4}$ of the couplets. Toward the end of the anthem, sandwiched in between a very folklike phrase in $\frac{6}{4}$ and the final Hallelujah section, there is a simple psalm tune in Common Meter.

A much more elaborate rondo is "The beauty of Israel," the refrain of which is Example 150. The texture of this anthem is more nearly normal for Billings, with predominant four-voice chorus, varied by one duet, one short solo, and one insignificant fuguing passage. It has a change of signature, for one section, from F minor to F major, and there are three indicated metrical changes, together with an implied change shown in Example 11.

A still more complicated structure is found in another anthem for Fast Day, "Sanctify a fast." Its first part, descriptive of a drought, is in G minor, and the form is approximately A B A'. Then the key changes to G major, to indicate the jubilation at the coming of the rains. Here, after an introductory section, there is a sort of refrain, to the words, "Be glad, then, ye children of Zion . . . the former and the latter rain in the first month." The refrain is of tremendous length (twenty-two bars in its shortest version) and it is varied considerably each time it returns, the variation being especially marked on the word "rejoice." The four appearances of the refrain are separated by brief couplets for solo voices. Thus the form of the latter half of this anthem resembles both the rondo and the variation.

While considering the formal structure in Billings' anthems, it may be well to pause a moment to note what Macdougall says about it. He comments witheringly as follows: "In writing longer compositions than psalm-tunes he may not have had the idea that an anthem, for example, was simply a number of psalm-tunes, one after the other; but there is nothing in his anthems, looking at their structure, inconsistent with this idea. . . . When Billings and his followers attempted pieces where it was necessary to have some form in order to hold the music together, they always failed completely."[22]

The anthem which Macdougall has chosen to illustrate Billings' alleged weakness in form is *Universal Praise* ("O praise God"), an anthem which contains an exuberant, doggerel text. (See p. 10) He complains that of the anthem's ten sections, each section comes "to a dead stop with the authentic cadence in C major." This is true enough, and there is without question monotony of key and of harmony. A large part of the harmonic monotony here stems from Billings' unnaturally chaste style, almost devoid of parallel fifths, for a wonder, and abounding in tonics and dominants! One should add, however, that this anthem bears no resemblance whatever to an assemblage of psalm tunes.

What Macdougall failed to grasp was that, although *Universal Praise* is not one of Billings' best anthems, it is constructed impeccably. Six of the ten sections end with exactly the same music, to the words, "Praise the Lord" (Example 192), thus

192.

Praise, praise, praise, praise, praise the Lord.

making the whole an extended litany in rondo form. The final section is a coda in $\frac{3}{2}$ to the words, "Amen, hallelujah." This is one of seven changes of meter (Macdougall grudgingly admits of "one or two") which afford variety, and there is also a fair amount of variety of texture.

[22] Macdougall, *op. cit.*, p. 57.

If anywhere, one might expect to find examples of Macdougall's *bête noire,* the anthem as a set of psalm tunes, among
the rare Billings anthems that are entirely in verse than among
those with prose or mixed texts. (Actually, the homophonic
psalm tune introduced into "I will love thee" is unique in Billings' anthems.) There are two short hymn anthems in the
Suffolk Harmony: "Lift up your eyes" and "O clap your hands."
In the former anthem the first stanza is set in a somewhat florid
¾ and the second stanza in 6/4 with contrast in both meter and
texture. The latter anthem, although in 4/4 for both stanzas, is also
florid for the first stanza and more direct for the second. Pope's
popular hymn, "Vital spark of heavenly flame," lends itself so
admirably to descriptive touches that in Billings' setting there
is not the slightest suggestion of the conventional psalm tune.

A fourth hymn anthem, "The Lord descended," is different
from all the others, for its text consists of one eight-line stanza,
which is then repeated twice, with a rather elaborate Hallelujah
section at the end. In the first setting of the text the cadences are
alternately dominant and tonic, and the same is true of the second and third settings. Even more, in five of the six dominant
cadences the tenor sings D, and in all of the tonic cadences he
sings C, once in the lower octave. Thus, although there are considerable contrasts in meter and in style among the three strophes,
there is a strong sense of unity; so much so that the whole can
be construed as a theme with variations plus a coda. (Examples 23
and 24 show two versions of part of the text of this anthem.)

While considering variation form, one should not forget Billings' excellent Christmas carol, *Shiloh* (Example 156), in which
the second half of the melody is a triple-meter variant of the first
half. Then, too, there is the *Lamentation Over Boston,* which was
analyzed as a free chaconne on page 110. At the opposite pole
from those anthems in which unity is gained through repetition,
are those such as *David's Lamentation* which are so short that no
formal design is needed for their appreciation. The concluding
bars of this anthem were presented in Example 17.

It would be foolish to deny that in some of Billings' sectionalized anthems the whole is less than the sum of its parts. The
Charity Anthem, "Blessed is he," in NEPS, has variety of meter,

texture, and key, but the parts are uninteresting in themselves. Worth noting on the final page is a good example of triplets opposing duplets and one of the three trills in all of Billings' anthems. Billings must have been rightly dissatisfied with his setting, for he used the greater part of this text in an anthem with the same incipit in PSA. But, despite some folklike melody (Example 50), the effect of the whole is little better than in the former version.

One of the dubious distinctions of the earlier "Blessed is he," in C major, is its complete lack of accidentals, save for a lone B natural in the middle section in C minor. In the same collection, "As the hart" begins in G minor and comprises three sections in G minor and three in G major. But it too does not have a single accidental. Nor does "Hear my prayer," which is in A minor. The lack of accidentals is less surprising in the remaining two anthems in this collection, "The Lord descended" and "The Lord is King," since both are in C major. It has been noted earlier in this book that many more accidentals must have been intended in the anthems and psalm tunes of NEPS than appeared in print, but Billings' inexperience in writing music resulted in the single B natural in the five anthems.

By the time that his last work, CH, came to fruition, Billings had had plenty of experience in writing accidentals. But three of its anthems are also completely devoid of accidentals, an indication either that these were earlier anthems not previously printed or else that Billings had not wholly lost his dislike of modulation. All in C major, these three anthems are: "I will love thee," "I charge you," and "The heavens declare." In another late work, SH, the anthem, "Behold how good," is in C without accidentals, and "Lift up your eyes," in F major, has one B natural, escaping several others by a change of key signature to C. Several of the anthems mentioned in this paragraph and the preceding one are among Billings' most pleasing creations. It is something of a feat to overcome the handicap of a complete lack of modulation!

It is not strange that six of the anthems without accidentals should have been in C major, for it is Billings' favorite key, used also in ten anthems *with* accidentals. But Billings also employed many other keys. If one includes all the different keys in the anthems that were indicated by key signatures rather than by accidentals (if an anthem was in G minor, with a middle section in G major, each key is listed once), there are a total of 65 signatures, divided among fourteen keys as follows: *major keys,* F, 6; C, 16; G, 5; A, 4; E, 3; B, 2; F sharp, 1; *minor keys,* F, 4; C, 4; G, 6; A, 7; E, 3; B, 3; F sharp, 1. A similar census has been taken of the psalm tunes in Billings' six collections—not too accurate, for it includes repeated tunes except for those in MM. The 270 items are divided thus: *major keys,* E flat, 10; B flat, 6; F, 27; C, 48; G, 34; D, 26; A, 10; E, 6; *minor keys,* F, 4; C, 9; G, 13; D, 11; A, 40; E, 1; B, 7; F sharp, 8. The absence of both D major and D minor from the anthem list is the only anomaly in what otherwise represents an interestingly wide range of tonal centers.

If it seems odd that Billings used minor keys with two, three, and four flats more extensively than their related majors, it must be remembered that for him the minor mode usually included the relative major as an integral part, although the major mode was as closely linked to the supertonic minor as to the relative minor. The most remote minor key that was touched upon in the anthems was C sharp minor, which occurred in "Blessed is he" (Example 110) and also in "We have heard with our ears." The latter (*Psalm 44*) is a long and excellent sectionalized anthem, having transitions also to the dominant key of B major and a middle section in E minor, where there are some D sharps and even a Picardy third. There are Picardy thirds, by the way, on the final chord of "Hear, O Heaven" and in several places of "O God, thou hast been displeased," as well as one in "Be glad then, America" shortly after a Dorian sixth. *Psalm 44* has the usual variety of tempo and meter, including some wrong barring in the expressive middle section. (Example 37) There are nine short solo passages, the anthem beginning with Example 46. The amount of variety present would not in itself offset the frequent tonic cadences. But the attractive melodies hold the listener's attention throughout, making this one of the best of Billings' longer anthems. To deny the validity of the sectionalized anthem, as Macdougall and other writers have done, is precisely the same and just as stupid as it would be to deny the validity of the classic suite on the ground that it has too many movements and all of them in the tonic key!

But, even if the sectionalized anthem does have validity as an art form, it is seldom that Billings was as happy in the end result as he was in "We have heard with our ears." Two other anthems of approximately its length (six or seven minutes) can be highly recommended: "Sanctify a fast" and "O thou to whom." Among those of medium length (about four minutes), "The beauty of Israel" and "The Lord descended" are attractive. But the real gems are the miniatures, such as the well-known *David's Lamentation, The Rose of Sharon*, "I charge you," and "Sing ye merrily." Here the changes of texture, meter, and key are sufficiently frequent as to be interesting, but not so frequent as to be confusing.

Much the same may be said about the texture of Billings' psalm tunes. In a tune of ordinary length, the inclusion of a single solo or duet makes a pleasing break, as in *Savannah* (Example 182) or *Sudbury* (Example 184), just as a concluding section of fuguing is grateful. But even in *Rochester*, with its two initial duets (Example 135), the atmosphere begins to get somewhat artificial. And certainly a splendid tune like *Emanuel* (Example 58) is hindered rather than helped by its multiplicity of textural elements. The short, irregular ejaculations in the prose text of an anthem often lend themselves admirably to a responsorial type of treatment which may be quite unsuitable for the more regular phrasing of a metrical text.

Three-quarters of Billings' psalm tunes are neither responsive nor fuguing. These include such infectious melodies as *Boston* (Example 51), *Conquest* (Example 52), and *Baltimore* (Example 59), while only an initial duet prevents *Judea* (Example 57) from being in the same class. *Shiloh* (Example 56), on the other hand, is a tune like *Emanuel*, with its texture changing a half dozen times. Its excellent melody, however, lies in the tenor throughout, and it surmounts the handicap of over-varied texture.

And so, in general, the part played by textural changes in Billings' psalm tunes is insignificant. In the anthems it plays a much more important part; but, as we have seen, it becomes more effective when combined with unifying recurrence, as in rondo or variation form.

In conclusion, it is not nearly so necessary to go about making apologies for Billings as some people seem to think. Chauvinism is something that natives of other countries can understand and will make allowances for; a reverse chauvinism makes no sense to either the native or the foreigner. Let me make the categorical assertion, which unfortunately cannot be completely demonstrated with the aid of a couple of hundred examples, that Billings was a much better composer than any of the English composers performed in 18th-century America, just as he was superior to his younger contemporaries in the New England school. (Daniel prefers Oliver Holden, whose style, however, was not sufficiently more polished than Billings' to compensate for his harmonic and rhythmic flabbiness.) This is not to say that he was a great or even a near-great composer; it perhaps does imply that he had more genuis than talent, if one wishes to make a distinction between these words.

Perhaps the key to the interest that Billings holds for many of us today is his enthusiasm—an enthusiasm reflected in the texts chosen so carefully and so greatly enhanced by his own additions; an enthusiasm that led him to forge rhythms that slipped out of the dance and the four-bar phrase, to the consternation of slow-witted traditionalists of our day; an enthusiasm that, by insisting that all the voices have melodies to sing, earned for his harmonies the frequent commentary—harsh, archaic, uncouth—a condemnation that may now appear an accolade; an enthusiasm expressed in the festooned jubilations that sometimes pass beyond the formal-garden style of Handel and his Italian peers and approach the cantillations of the Hebrews whose sacred poetry he understood so well; an enthusiasm that might have taken for its motto his own bicephalous text: "Is any of you merry let him sing psalms, singing and making melody in your hearts to the Lord." (*James* 5: 13; *Ephesians* 5: 19)

There are those among our contemporary composers in America who strive, ever so self-consciously, to be primitive and down-to-earth, and perhaps they may deceive foreigners into considering them the real thing. William Billings needs no qualification: his music was not without roots, as we have tried so carefully to document; but what he himself contributed, with lyric spontaneity and dramatic power, made him a representative American of whom we can be very proud.

Alphabetical Index of Billings' Psalm Tunes

The numbers after the titles give the location of the tunes in the various Billings collections. Boldface numbers designate the extra tunes in SH and in the variant edition of PSA; italics, the "additional" tunes in the latter edition. In the variant edition, *The Bird* and *The Lark* are laid in without pagination. An asterisk following a number denotes a longer version of a tune (often with fuguing) than that appearing in another volume or volumes. The repetition of a title indicates that two different tunes had been given the same name. The abbreviated poetic meters are familiar, with the possible exception of HM for Hallelujah Meter (666688). The tune *Savannah* is in amphibrachs and so should not be classified as LM, although it has eight syllables in each line. The fairly common meter designated as 8's 6 l might be called LM 6 l. However, its rhyme scheme is aabccb, which has little connection with LM. Double, triple, and even quadruple meters are found and are differentiated by an extra initial. If a doubled meter occurs only in the longer version of a tune, the D is put in brackets.

Title	NEPS	SMA	MM	PSA	SH	CH	Poetic Meter	Example
Adams						153	HM	
Adoration			79				LM	
Africa	14	4	4				CM	107
Albany	17						CM	
America	1	5	21				8's 6 l	
Amherst	48	7	11				HM	
Andover	65						CM	
Andover				78			CM	
Ashford	89						CM	36
Ashham			40				LM	
Asia	60						SM	
Asia			26				SM	
Assurance				8			CM	

Title	NEPS	SMA	MM	PSA	SH	CH	Poetic Meter	Example
Attleborough	59						SM	
Aurora		1*	11				SM	
Baptism					37		887887224448	
Baltimore		47					5656664	59
Barre	67						CM	
Bellingham						58	CM	
Beneficence					10		LMD	
Benevolence		72					CM	
Berlin				3			LMD	
Bethlehem		69*	17				CM[D]	166
Bird, The				NP			CM	
Bolton		25					HM	
Boston	23	2					CMD	51
Braintree	43						8's 6 l	
Brattle Square					10		CM	
Brattle Street	19						LMD	
Brattle Street					19		LM	
Brest			4				LM	
Bridgwater	40						LM	
Broad Cove						129	CM	
Brookfield	7	4	22				LM	
Brookline	2		7				CM	
Brunswick		8					CM	
Burlington					49		76767876	
Calvary			29				CM	
Cambridge	47	13	20				8's 6 l	181
Camden					14		LMD	
Charleston	15						CMD	
Chelsea	48						LM	
Chelsea					48		5556 D	
Chester	91	12	12				LM	
Chesterfield	63						CM	176
Chocksett		49	10				HM	
Claremont						154	886886	
Cobham						185	CM	
Cohasset						59	LM	
Columbia		56	14				HM	
Concord	5						CM	
Connection		99	24				SM	
Conquest					44		8787 Ref	52

Title	NEPS	SMA	MM	PSA	SH	CH	Poetic Meter	Example
Consolation		19					CM	
Corsica	46						CM	
Creation			3			52*	CM[D]	85,106
Cross Street						56	8's 61	
Crucifixion			7	1	5*		LM	
Cumberland	16						CM	
Danbury			27	3			SM	
Dedham	45						LM	
Dedham						95	LM	
Delaware			28	4			LM	
Dickinson	73						SM	
Dighton	70						CM	
Dorchester	78	9					CM	67
Dublin			26				SM	
Dudley			6				LM	
Dunstable		100*	23				CM	
Duxborough	8	3	9				LM	
Eastham	62						CM	
East Sudbury						152	HM	
East Town	63						SM	178
Eden					56		CM	
Egypt						61	CM	
18th Psalm	80						CM	
Election					40		11 6 6 11 11	
Emanuel				46			11's	58
Emmaus		20	29				LM	
Essex	65						SM	
Europe	90*		5	4			CM	9
Exeter		41					CM	
Fairfield	13						SM	
Fitchburgh			3	2			LM	
Framingham			3	4*			SM	104
Franklin			6				LM	
Freedom	58						SM	
Friendship	61						SM	
Georgia	76						LM	
Georgia			31				LM	
Gilead						82	CM	
Gloucester					47		6 6 4 5 5 10	
Golgotha				61			CMD	

Title	NEPS	SMA	MM	PSA	SH	CH	Poetic Meter	Example
Great Plain						47	LM	93
Greenland	21						SM	
Halifax		23	17				10's 6 l	
Hampshire	3						LM	
Hampshire			28	6			CM	
Hampton	14						LM	
Hanover	75						LM	177
Hanover New	75						CM	
Hartford				103	25		85857785	
Harvard	68						CM	
Hatfield					5		CMD	113
Haverhill	96						CM	
Heath		11					LM	
Hebron	69	16	14				SM	111
Hingham	6						SM	
Holden	88						8's 6 l	
Hollis	86						LM	
Hollis Street	94	16					10 10 11 11	
Hopkinton						144	8787 Ref	
Hull					46		886886	
Invocation						57	LM	
Ipswich	72						CM	
Jamaica	64						LM	
Jamaica			4	7			CM	
Jargon		102					8787	138
Jerusalem				42			77775777	
Jordan				6	33		CMD	
Judea		6					CMT	57,161
Kittery					12		CM	
Lancaster	93						LM	173
Lark, The			NP				LM	
Lebanon	95	14	9				CM	1
Lewis Town						198	CMT	
Lexington	66						LM	
Liberty	9						SM	
Lincoln	77						SM	
Lynn	70						CM	
Madrid			32*	2*	24		10 10 11 11	
Majesty			68				CMD	160
Malden	4						LM	

Title	*NEPS*	*SMA*	*MM*	*PSA*	*SH*	*CH*	Poetic Meter	Example
Manchester			5	6*			LM[D]	
Mansfield			30	3			8's 6 l	
Marblehead	71	14					CM	65
Marshfield	76	15	23				LM	
Maryland		29*	13				SM	108
Massachusetts	40						10 10 11 11	
Medfield	94	10					LM	
Medford	86						LM	
Medway		18					CM	
Mendom					53	27	76767876	
Middlesex	62						CM	
Middleton	74						SM	
Milton	44						CM	74
Moravia					50		11 11 10 11 11 11	
Moriah					39		10's	
Morning Hymn						68	CM	83
Morpheus			8				LM	
Nantasket	41						LM	
Nantucket	2						SM	
Nazareth			6				CM	
New Boston	6						HM	174
Newburn			28				CM	
New Castle			4				CM	
New Hingham	59	15	16				SM	179
New North	69	67	15				CM	167
New Plymouth						169	CMD	
Newport	87						LM	
New South	12	10	9				SM	
New Town	3						LM	
Norfolk						51	LM	
Northborough					17		886886	
North Providence		71					CM	101
North River	16						CM	7
Number 45	74						HM	
Nutfield	68						SM	
Old Brick	20						LM	
Old North	22						SMD	
Old South	21						CM	2
Orange Street	42						CM	

Title	NEPS	SMA	MM	PSA	SH	CH	Poetic Meter	Example
Orleans	77						CM	
Oxford			27				8's 6 l	
Paris			31				LM	
Pembroke	5						LM	
Pembroke New	10						8's 6 l	
Petersburgh				28			LMD	70
Philadelphia		51*	20				SM	168
Philanthropy					36		8 8 8 8 10 10	
Phoebus	39						CMD	112
Pitt	57						SMD	
Plainfield	93						CM	
Pleasant Street	41						LM	
Plymton	11						8's 6 l	
Pomfret	7						CM	
Pownall	67						LM	
Princetown	45	17	22				CM	
Providence	78						LM	
Pumpily	60	24	16				HM	
Purchase Street	73						SM	
Purchase Street			7				LM	
Queen Street	50						CMD	
Redemption			22				8868886	
Resignation				62			CMD	
Restoration					35		4446624446	
Resurrection					7		7's with Hal	
Revelation			29			62*	CM	
Richmond		50		23			787878	
Rochester						81	10 10 11 11	135
Rocky Nook						49	CM	
Roxbury	20						LM	
Roxbury		46	24				10 10 11 11	
Rutland				48			LMD	
St. Andrew's						184	CM	
St. Elisha's	8						LM	
St. Enoch						67	CM	94
St. John's						55	LM	
St. Thomas						127	CMQ	
Sapphic Ode	108	21					11 11 11 5	
Savannah		3					8's	182
Saybrook			30				LM	

Title	NEPS	SMA	MM	PSA	SH	CH	Poetic Meter	Example
Scituate	9						LM	
Sharon		32					CM	40
Sherburne		43	12				668668	
Shiloh					1		CMD	56
Shirley	74						LM	
Sinai					45		8's 6 l	
Smithfield	92						CM	
South Boston						83	HM	
Spain		42	13				668668	
Stockbridge		44					LMT	6
Stoughton	42						CM	
Sturbridge				5			LM	
Sudbury	12						CM	
Sudbury						69	SMD	184
Suffolk	17	17	25				LM	
Sullivan		9					LM	
Summer Street	66						LM	
Sunday		54					LM	41
Swanzey	72						CM	
Taunton	49						CM	
Thomas Town				2		66	CMD	
Tower Hill	58						CM	
Trinity New			32				CM	
Union	4						SM	64
Unity	18						LM	
Uxbridge	64						CM	
Vermont		55					CMD	117
Victory						170	CM	
Waltham	95	20	10				SM	
Wareham			31	51*			SM	
Warren		62					7's	
Washington		79					LM	
Washington Street						64	CM	
Water Town	13						LM	
Wellfleet	61						SM	180
West Boston				41			7's D	
Westfield	71						LM	
West Sudbury						50	CMD	
Weymouth						74	SM	

Title	NEPS	SMA	MM	PSA	SH	CH	Poetic Meter	Example
Wheeler's Point	18						LM	
Wheeler's Point					21		CM	
Wilkes	80						LM	
Williamsburgh	87						CM	
Worcester		48					CMD	
Wrentham		28	15				10 10 10 10 11 11	

APPENDIX B

Index of Billings' Anthems by Texts
With Cross References to Titles and Occasions

Incipit	Source of Incipit	Location of Anthem	Title or Occasion	Examples
And I saw	Rev. 5	PSA 35		
As the hart	Ps. 42	NEPS 31	Ps. 42	91, 100
Behold, how good	Ps. 133	SH 3	Union, Ps. 133	

(Be glad then, America. See "Mourn, mourn")

Blessed is he	Ps. 41	NEPS 97	Charity	
Blessed is he	Ps. 41	PSA 24	Charity	50, 110
By the rivers of Watertown	Ps. 137	SMA 33	Lamentation Over Boston	21, 152, 153, 154

(Charity. See "Blessed is he")
(Christmas. See "Hark, hark, hear you not?")
(Communion. See "Let every mortal ear")
(David's Lamentation. See "David the king")

David the king	II Sam. 18	SMA 22	David's Lamentation	17

(Deliverance. See "I will love thee")
(Easter. See "The Lord is risen indeed")
(Euroclydon. See "They that go down")
(Fast. See "Hear, hear, O heavens," "Hear my prayer," "Mourn, mourn," "Sanctify a fast," and "The heavens declare")
(Funeral. See "I heard a great voice" and "Samuel the priest")
(Forefathers' Landing. See "We have heard")
(Gratitude. See "I love the Lord")

Hark, hark, hear you not?		CH 117	Christmas	
Hear, hear, O heavens	Isa. 1	CH 42	Fast	190
Hear my prayer	Ps. 143	NEPS 81	Fast	14
Hear my prayer	Ps. 39	SMA 26	Ps. 39	62
I am come	Sol. Song 5	CH 76		
I am the rose	Sol. Song 2	SMA 73	(The Rose of Sharon)	149

147

Incipit	Source of Incipit	Location of Anthem	Title or Occasion	Examples
I charge you	Sol. Song 2	CH 155		87, 88
I heard a great voice	Rev. 14	SMA 52	Funeral	43
I love the Lord	Ps. 116	SMA 63	Gratitude, Ps. 116	29

(Independence. See "The states, O Lord")

Is any afflicted	James 5	SMA 30		47, 61
I will love thee	Ps. 18	CH 131	Deliverance	78

(Lamentation Over Boston. See "By the rivers of Watertown")

Let every mortal ear	Isa. 55 (Watts)	PSA 89	Communion	49, 54
Lift up your eyes	Watts	SH 30		

(Mariners. See "They that go down")

Mourn, mourn	(Joel 2)	CH 145	Fast (Be glad, then, America)	
My friends, I am going	Billings	CH 164	Dying Christian's Last Farewell	
O clap your hands	Ps. 47	SH NP	Thanksgiving, Ps. 47	
O God, my heart is fixed	Ps. 108	CH 176	Thanksgiving, Ps. 108	
O God, thou hast been	Ps. 60	CH 138	Variety Without Method	144
O praise God	Ps. 150	CH 97	Universal Praise, Thanksgiving	86, 192
O praise the Lord	Ps. 148	CH 35	Thanksgiving	

(Ordination. See "O thou to whom")

O thou to whom	Ps. 8 (NV)	CH 105	Ordination	48, 96, 134

(Psalm 18. See "The Lord descended")
(Psalm 19. See "The heavens declare")
(Psalm 39. See "Hear my prayer")
(Psalm 42. See "As the hart")

Incipit	Source of Incipit	Location of Anthem	Title or Occasion	Examples
(Psalm 44. See "We have heard")				
(Psalm 47. See "O clap your hands")				
(Psalm 81. See "Sing ye merrily")				
(Psalm 93. See "The Lord is king")				
(Psalm 107. See "They that go down")				
(Psalm 108. See "O God, my heart is fixed")				
(Psalm 116. See "I love the Lord")				
(Psalm 126. See "When the Lord")				
(Psalm 133. See "Behold, how good")				
(Retrospect. See "Was not the day?")				
Samuel the priest	I. Sam. 25	SH 52	Funeral	22
Sanctify a fast	Joel 1	CH 186	Fast	127
Sing praises to the Lord	Ps. 30	CH 70	Thanksgiving	
Sing ye merrily	Ps. 81	SMA 57	Ps. 81	19
(Sublimity. See "The heavens declare")				
(Thanksgiving. See "O clap your hands," "O God, my heart is fixed," "O praise God," "O praise the Lord," "Sing praises to the Lord," "The heavens declare," and "We have heard")				
The beauty of Israel	II Sam. 1	PSA 16		11, 137, 150
(The Dying Christian to His Soul. See "Vital spark")				
The heavens declare	Ps. 19	CH 171	Sublimity, Thanksgiving, Fast, Ps. 19	
The Lord descended	Ps. 18 (OV)	NEPS 51	Ps. 18	23, 24, 76
The Lord is king	Ps. 93	NEPS 24	Ps. 93	12, 35, 145
The Lord is risen indeed	Luke 24	SH Sup 1	Easter	63
(The Rose of Sharon. See "I am the rose")				
The states, O Lord	Billings	SMA 91	Independence	175
They that go down	Ps. 107	PSA 53	Euroclydon, Mariners, Ps. 107	147, 148
Thou, O God	Ps. 65	PSA 9		79, 136, 140
(Union. See "Behold, how good")				
(Universal Praise. See "O praise God")				

Incipit	Source of Incipit	Location of Anthem	Title or Occasion	Examples
(Variety Without Method. See "O God, thou hast been")				
Vital spark	Pope	PSA 99	The Dying Christian to His Soul	
Was not the day?	Billings	SMA 81	Retrospect	44, 45, 60
We have heard	Ps. 44	CH 84	Forefathers' Landing, Thanksgiving, Ps. 44	37, 46, 151
When the Lord	Ps. 126	CH 160	Ps. 126	92
Who is this?	Isa. 63	PSA 63		139

APPENDIX C

Selective Index of Billings' Psalm Tunes by Texts

First Line	Poet	Tune	Examples
Ah, lovely appearance of death	C. Wesley	Savannah	182
All is hush	James Relly	Jerusalem	
All over lovely	John Relly	Moriah	
And must this body die	Watts	Maryland	108
As shepherds in Jewry	Trad.	Emanuel	58
A virgin unspotted	Trad.	Judea	57, 161
Awake my heart, arise my tongue	Watts	Andover	
Blessed is the man	C. Wesley	Hanover	177
Come, let us join	Watts	North Providence	101
Death, O the awful sound	Unknown	New Hingham	179
Death with his warrant	Unknown	Lebanon	1
Father of mercies	Unknown	Baltimore	59
From all that dwell	Watts	Stockbridge	6
Glorious Jesus	James Relly	Hartford	113
God bless our gracious king	Trad.	Liberty	
Greatly beloved	James Relly	Restoration	
Here is a song	Peck	West Sudbury	
How glorious is our	Watts	Sharon	40
How pleased and blest	Watts	Spain	
How vast must their	T. & B.	Marblehead	65
In vain we lavish out	Watts	Vermont	117
Jesus Christ is risen today	Anon	Resurrection	
Jesus, thy name we praise	James Relly	Glocester	
Let differing nations join	T. & B.	Philadelphia	168
Let every mortal ear	Watts	Europe	9
Let horrid Jargon	Unknown	Jargon	138
Let others boast	Watts	Hatfield	113
Let tyrants shake	Billings	Chester	
(Let Whig and Tory	Unknown	Europe	9)

151

First Line	Poet	Tune	Examples
Lord, in the morning	Watts	Phoebus	112
Majestic God, when I descry		Sunday	41
Methinks I see a heavenly host	Billings	Boston	51
Methinks I see a heavenly host	Billings	Shiloh	56
My belovèd, haste away	James Relly	Richmond	
My God, my life, my love	Watts	Hebron	111
Not all the powers on earth	Unknown	Columbia	
Not to our names	Watts	Halifax	
Now shall my inward joy	Watts	Africa	107
O how doth God	James Relly	Baptism	
O Love, what a secret	James Relly	Moravia	
O praise the Lord	T. & B.	New North	167
O praise ye the Lord	T. & B.	Roxbury	
Rejoice, the Lord is King	C. Wesley	Bolton	
Shall Wisdom cry aloud	Watts	Framingham	104
Shepherds, rejoice	Watts	Boston	51
Sing to the Lord a new-made song	T. & B.	St. Enoch	94
Sing the triumphs	James Relly	Conquest	52
Th' Eternal speaks	Unknown	Redemption	
The God of Glory	Watts	Wrentham	
The Lord descended	S. & H.	Majesty	160
The Lord himself	Unknown	Ashford	36
The Lord my pasture	Addison	Cross Street	
Thee will I laud	Unknown	Milton	74
Thou art my blest	John Relly	Election	
Thus saith the high	Watts	Petersburgh	70
Time, what an empty	Watts	Dorchester	67
To God, the mighty Lord	T. & B.	Amherst	
What beauties divine	James Relly	Chelsea	
What if the saint	Peck	Sudbury	184
When I with pleasing	Watts	Creation	85, 106
When the fierce North-wind	Watts	Sapphic Ode	

First Line	Poet	Tune	Examples
While shepherds watched	Tate	Bethlehem	166
Ye servants of God	C. Wesley	Rochester	135
Ye slumbering saints	Watts	Great Plain	93
Ye that delight	T. & B.	Cambridge	181

No texts were printed for the following six tunes, all in NEPS, from which examples have been taken:

Tune	Example
Chesterfield	176
East Town	178
Lancaster	173
New Boston	174
North River	7
Old South	2

APPENDIX D

Index of Non-Billings' Psalm Tunes

Title	Location	Poetic Meter	Examples
Ashfield	Shumway 94	8787	10
Barnstable	Read 32	7's D	33
Chesterton	Tans'ur 19	CM	170
Coronation	Holden 89	CM	185
Cranly	Adams 20	CM	162
Derby	Adams 2	CM	5, 125
Derby	Lyon 29	SM	171
Dishley	Arnold 36	CM	99
Dorchester	Tans'ur 13	CM	28
Dunchurch	Tans'ur 2	CM	169
Freetown	Read 34	HM	124
Garenton	Arnold 44	CM	34
Greensleeves	Traditional	87876867	53
Greenville	Common Use	878787	129a
Hadlow	Adams 62	8's 6 l	189
Hamburg	Common Use	LM	172
Hartford	Law 56	LMD	141
Hoeton	Arnold 48	CM	122
Holy Manna	Walker 103	8787 D	129
Knighton	Knapp 146	CM	68
Leeds	Law 15	LM	69
Lenox	Walker 77	HM	103
Loughborough	Arnold 11	CM	39, 126
Middleton	Laus Deo 47	7's D	188
Naples	Read 28	LM	143
Pembrook	Read 62	SM	183
Pennsylvania	Shumway 154	LM	84
Psalm 3	Laus Deo 23	CM	102
Psalm 5	Lyon 42	CM	115, 119
Psalm 9	Lyon 45	CM	187
Psalm 21	Jocelyn 67	CM	186
Psalm 23	Lyon 50	866866	81
Psalm 113	Scot. Psal. xii	8's 12 l	98
Psalm 136	Lyon 80	HM	75
Psalm 139	Frost 191	CMD	97

Title	Location	Poetic Meter	Examples
Ryall	Tans'ur 29	CM	114
St. Martin's	Common Use	CM	66
Shepshead	Arnold 39	CM	82, 142
Shoreham	Adams 74	LM	73
Southwell	Church 48	SM	146
Stanford	Arnold 18	CM	131
Thrussington	Arnold 58	CMD	3, 4
Uppingham	Tans'ur 27	CM	15
Wales	Shumway 152	LM	42
Wells	Tans'ur 81	LM	32
Wendover	Adams 39	CMD	120
Winter	Read 33	CM	163
Wirksworth	Lyon 25	SM	8
Wrotham	Adams 28	CM	130

APPENDIX E

Index of Non-Billings' Anthems by Texts

First Line	Source of Text	Location	Composer	Examples
Arise, shine	Isa. 60	Law 85	Williams	133
Behold, I bring you	Luke 2	Law 75	Stephenson	27
Bring unto the Lord	Ps. 29	Knapp 39	Knapp	95
Give the king thy judgments (*The King's Anthem*)	Ps. 72	Tans'ur 49	Knapp	113
I was glad	Ps. 122	Stickney 165	Williams	13, 16
I will sing unto the Lord	Exod. 15	Knapp 32	Knapp	71
Jehovah reigns	Ps. 97	Stickney 189	Tuckey	89
Let the shrill trumpet's	Ps. 150 (N.V.)	Lyon 165	Lyon	80
O be joyful	Ps. 100	Holden 148	Selby	90
O be joyful	Ps. 100	Read 17	Read	20
O clap your hands	Ps. 47	Law 78	West	25
O clap your hands	Ps. 47	Tans'ur 60	Tans'ur	18, 77
O Lord our governor	Ps. 8	Law 66	West	66, 128
O praise the lord of heaven	Ps. 148	Tans'ur 57	Tans'ur	30
O praise the Lord, O my soul	Ps. 104	Tans'ur 74	Tans'ur	31
O sing unto the Lord	Ps. 96	French 93	French	164
Praise ye the Lord	Ps. 149	Laus Deo 109	Gram	132
Sing, O ye heavens	Isa. 44	Law 90	Stephenson	155

First Line	Source of Text	Location	Composer	Examples
Sing, O ye heavens	Isa. 44	Shumway 18	Holden	72
The voice of my beloved	Sol. Song 2	Brownson 42	Swan	156
Unto us a child	Isa. 9	Flagg 5	Knapp	38
Vital spark (*Claremont*)	Pope	Walker 183	(Harwood)	55

Source of Secular Examples

Example 116. Fellowes' *The English Madrigal School*, Vol. 9, p. 34.

Example 121. *Ibid.*, Vol. 2, p. 18.

Example 157. Machaut Edition, 3. Band, *Motetten*. Motette 6; final cadence, p. 26.

Example 158. *Ibid.*, Motette 3; final cadence, p. 12.

Example 165. Parrish and Ohl's *Masterpieces*, p. 42.

BIBLIOGRAPHY. PART I

Books and Articles

Brady, Nicholas and Nahum Tate. *A New Version of the Psalms of David*, London, The Company of Stationers, 1711.

Chase, Gilbert. *America's Music From the Pilgrims to the Present*, New York, McGraw-Hill, 1955.

Church of England Psalter.

Daniel, Ralph Thomas. *The Anthem in New England Before 1800*, Harvard Dissertation, February, 1955.

Dinneen, William. *William Billings 1746-1800. The Psalm-Tunes and Fuging Pieces*, Providence, Author's Typescript, 1950.

Elson, Louis C. *The National Music of America and Its Sources*, Boston, L. C. Page, 1900.

Fellowes, Edmund H. *English Cathedral Music*, 2nd ed., London, Methuen & Co., 1945.

Garrett, Allen McCain. *William Billings and the Fuguing Tune*, University of North Carolina Master's Dissertation, 1949.

Garrett, Allen McCain. *The Works of William Billings*, University of North Carolina Ph. D. Dissertation, 1952.

Goldberg, Isaac. "The First American Musician," *The American Mercury*, Vol. 14, 1928, pp. 67-75.

Grove's Dictionary of Music and Musicians, 5th ed., Eric Blom, London, Macmillan, 1954.

Holy Bible (King James Standard Version)

Howard, John Tasker. *Our American Music*, rev. ed., New York, Thomas Y. Crowell, 1939.

Julian, John. *A Dictionary of Hymnology*, rev. ed., London, J. Murray, 1907.

Lindstrom, Carl E. "William Billings and His Times," *Musical Quarterly*, Vol. 25, 1939, pp. 479-497.

Lowens, Irving. "The Origins of the American Fuging Tune," *Journal of the American Musicological Society*, Vol. 6, 1953, pp. 43-52.

Macdougall, Hamilton Crawford. *Early New England Psalmody*, Brattleboro, Stephen Daye Press, 1940.

Metcalf, Frank J. *American Writers and Compilers of Sacred Music*, New York, Abingdon Press, 1925.

Morin, Raymond. "A Pioneer in American Music," *The New England Quarterly*, Vol. 14, 1941, pp. 25-33.

Pierce, Edwin Hall. "The Rise and Fall of the 'Fugue-Tune' in America," *Musical Quarterly*, Vol. 16, 1930, pp. 214-228.
(Pope, Alexander). *The Complete Poetical Works of Alexander Pope*, New York, Thomas Y. Crowell, 1887.
Relly, James and John. *Christian Hymns, Poems, and Spiritual Songs*, Burlington, Isaac Collins, 1776.
Scholes, Percy A. *The Oxford Companion to Music*, London, Oxford University Press, 1938.
Sternhold, Thomas and John Hopkins. *The Whole Book of Psalms*, London, The Company of Stationers, 1636.
Tate and Brady. See Brady-Tate.
Walker, Ernest. *A History of Music in England*, 3rd ed., Oxford, Clarendon Press, 1952.
Watts, Isaac. *Horae Lyricae*, 10th ed., New York, Hugh Gaine, 1762.
Watts, Isaac. *Hymns and Spiritual Songs*, London, John Lawrence, 1707.
Wesley, John and Charles. *Hymns and Sacred Poems*, 2nd ed., Bristol, F. Farley, 1745.
Whitefield, George. *A Collection of Hymns for Social Worship*, London, W. Strahan, 1753.
Young, Edward. *The Poetical Works of Edward Young*, London, W. Pickering, 1834.

BIBLIOGRAPHY. PART 2

Collections of Music

Adams, Abraham. *The Psalmist's New Companion*, 10th ed., London, C. & S. Thompson, 1775 (?).
Arnold, John. *Leicestershire Harmony*, London, the author, 1759.
Bayley, Daniel. *New Universal Harmony*, Newburyport, the author, 1773.
Billings, William. *The New-England Psalm-Singer*, Boston, Edes & Gill, 1770.
Billings, William. *The Singing-Master's Assistant*, Boston, Draper & Folsom, 1778.
Billings, William. *Music in Miniature*, Boston, the author, 1781.
Billings, William. *The Psalm-Singer's Amusement*, Boston, the author, 1781.
Billings, William. *The Suffolk Harmony*, Boston, the author, 1786.
Billings, William. *The Continental Harmony*, Boston, Thomas & Andrews, 1794.

Brownson, Oliver. *New Collection of Sacred Harmony*, Simsbury, the author, 1797.

Church, John. *An Introduction to Psalmody*, London, Walsh & Hare, 1723.

Fellowes, Edmund H. *The English Madrigal School*, Vol. 2, London, Stainer & Bell, 1913.

Fellowes, Edmund H. *The English Madrigal School*, Vol. 9, London, Stainer & Bell, 1916.

Fisher, William Arms. *Ye Olde New-England Psalm-Tunes, 1620-1820*, Boston, O. Ditson, 1930.

Flagg, Josiah. *A Collection of All Tans'ur's and a Number of Other Anthems*, Boston, the author, 1766 (?).

French, Jacob. *New American Melody*, Boston, J. Norman and Medway, the author, 1789.

Frost, Maurice. *English and Scottish Psalm and Hymn Tunes c. 1543-1677*, London, S.P.C.K. and Oxford University Press, 1953.

Geer, E. Harold. *Hymnal for Colleges and Schools*, New Haven, Yale University Press, 1956.

Goldman, Richard Franko and Roger Smith. *Landmarks of Early American Music 1760-1800*, New York, G. Schirmer, 1943.

Holden, Oliver. *American Harmony*, Boston, Thomas & Andrews, 1792.

Holden, Oliver. *Union Harmony*, Boston, Thomas & Andrews, 1793.

Hymns Ancient and Modern, Hist. ed., London, W. Clowes & Sons, 1909.

Jocelyn, Simeon. *The Chorister's Companion*, 2nd ed., New Haven, the author, 1788.

Knapp, William. *New Church Melody*, 4th ed., London, R. Baldwin, 1761.

Laus Deo! (*Worcester Collection*), 5th ed., Boston, Thomas & Andrews, 1794.

Law, Andrew. *Select Harmony*, Farmington, T. & S. Green, 1779.

Lowens, Irving. *Hartford Harmony*, Hartford, Hartford Seminary Foundation Bookstore, 1953.

Lyon, James. *Urania*, Philadelphia, W. Bradford, 1761.

Machaut, Gillaume de. *Musikalische Werke*, ed. Friedrich Ludwig, Leipzig, Breitkopf & Härtel, 1929.

Parrish, Carl and John F. Ohl. *Masterpieces of Music Before 1750*, New York, Norton, 1951.

Read Daniel. *The American Singing Book*, New Haven, Meigis, Brown and Dana, 1785.

Read Daniel. *Columbian Harmonist*, No. 3, New Haven, the author, 1795.

The Scottish Metrical Psalter of A.D. 1635, ed. Neil Livingston, Glasgow, Maclure & Macdonald, 1864.

Shumway, Nehemiah. *The American Harmony*, Philadelphia, J. M'Culloch, 1793.

Stickney, John. *The Gentleman and Lady's Musical Companion*, Newburyport, D. Bayley, 1774.

Tans'ur, William. *Royal Melody Complete*, 3rd ed., bound with Williams, *The American Harmony*.

Walker, William. *The Southern Harmony*, New ed., New York, Hastings House, 1854; facsimile ed., New York, Hastings House, 1939.

Williams, Aaron. *The American Harmony or The Universal Psalmist*, Newburyport, D. Bayley, 1769.

BIBLIOGRAPHY. PART 3

*Modern Octavo Editions
of Billings' Works*

Many of the older publications in this list are out of print. The cross references to authors are for works in Parts 1 and 2 of this Bibliography.

America. See Goldman-Smith.

Amherst. See Walker.

"A Virgin unspotted." See *Judea*.

Be glad then, America. Ed., C. Dickinson, New York, Music Press, 1940.

Broad Cove. See Fisher.

Chester. Ed., O. Daniel, Boston, Birchard, 1946; Shaw-Parker, New York, Lawson-Gould, 1954. See Fisher, Goldman-Smith, etc.

Consonance. Ed., H. T. David, New York, Music Press, 1947.

Creation. Ed., C. Dickinson, New York, Music Press, 1941.

Crucifixion. Ed., O. Daniel, New York, Mercury, 1951.

David's Lamentation. Ed., O. Daniel, Boston, Birchard, 1946; E. Siegmeister, New York, C. Fischer, 1950. See Fisher, Walker.

Easter Anthem. Ed., R. Shaw, New York, G. Schirmer, 1951. See Fisher W. Walker.

Emanuel. Ed., O. Daniel, Boston, Birchard, 1946.

Euroclydon. Ed., E. Siegmeister, New York, C. Fischer, 1950.

Europe. See Goldman-Smith.

"Fare you well." See *The Dying Christian's Last Farewell*.

Funeral Anthem. Ed., O. Daniel, Boston, Birchard, 1946. See W. Walker.

Gilead. See Pierce.

God's Mighty Wonders. See *Euroclydon.*

Hark! hark! hear you not? Ed., C. Dickinson, New York, Music Press, 1944.

"I am the Rose of Sharon." See *The Rose of Sharon.*

"I heard a great voice." See *Funeral Anthem.*

"I love the Lord." See R. T. Daniel.

"I will love thee, O Lord." See R. T. Daniel.

Jargon. Ed., O. Daniel, New York, Music Press, 1949. See Goldberg.

Jordan. Ed., I. Lowens, New York, E. B. Marks, 1954. See Geer.

Judea. Ed., C. Dickinson, New York, Music Press, 1940; O. Daniel, Boston, Birchard, 1949; W. Ehret, New York, Lawson-Gould, 1956.

Kittery. Ed., I. Lowens, New York, G. Schirmer, 1956.

Lamentation Over Boston. Ed., O. Daniel, New York, Music Press, 1949. See Fisher.

Madrid. See Lowens' *Hartford Harmony.*

Majesty. See Fisher.

Mendom. Ed., R. L. Sanders, New York, Galaxy, 1956.

Modern Music. Ed., H. T. David, New York, Music Press, 1947; W. Ehret, New York, Lawson-Gould, 1959. See Goldberg.

Morpheus. Ed., I. Lowens, New York, E. B. Marks, 1953.

My Redeemer. See *Mendom.*

Paris. Ed., I Lowens, New York, E. B. Marks, 1953. See Lowens' *Hartford Harmony.*

Resurrection. Ed., O. Daniel, New York, Mercury, 1951.

Retrospect. Ed., O. Daniel, New York, Music Press, 1949.

"Salvation, oh, the joyful sound" (*Gilead*). See Pierce.

Savannah. See W. Walker (there called *Union*).

Shiloh. Ed., O. Daniel, Boston, Birchard, 1943.

The Bird. Ed., O. Daniel, Boston, Birchard, 1943.

The Dying Christian's Last Farewell. Ed., O. Daniel, Boston, Birchard, 1946.

"The Lord is risen indeed." See *Easter Anthem.*

The Rose of Sharon. Ed., O. Daniel, New York, G. Schirmer, 1950; G. Read, New York, Lawson-Gould, 1959. See Fisher.

The Shepherd's Carol. See *Shiloh.*

"Time, what an empty vapor 'tis" (Broad Cove). See Fisher.

Washington. Ed., J. Behrend, Philadelphia, Elkan-Vogel, 1954.

When Jesus wept. Ed., C. Dickinson, New York, Music Press, 1940.

General Index

For Billings himself, Parts A, B, and C of the Appendix take the place of an index. In this index there are references to other poets, composers, editors, and authors, as well as to technical features of the music. The few compositions listed here do not duplicate titles or texts in Parts D and E of the Appendix.

accidentals, lack of, xiii, 21, 105, 111f, 120, 124, 135
"Ach, Jupiter," 7f
Adams, Abraham, xiv, 17f, 54, 70, 85, 88f, 91, 95, 113, 115, 124f, 127f, 130
Addison, Joseph, 2
Adeste fideles, 124
Aeolian mode, xvi, 15, 100, 102, 108
Ainsworth Psalter, 5
Allen, Nathan H., xii
amphibrachic meter, 5f, 47f
anapestic meter, 5, 43, 47
Anglican chant, 32
Anglo-Genevan Psalter, 3, 33, 68
anonymous composer, 46
anonymous texts, 2, 7
appogiaturas, 53, 87f, 95, 123
Arnold, John, xiv, 16f, 30, 34, 38, 59, 70, 89f, 92f, 95f, 103, 112f, 124f, 130
augmented sixth, 86f, 92
augmented triad, 85, 87, 115
Authorized (King James) Version, 9-12

Babcock, Samuel, 113
Bach, J. S., 128
Barry, John, xii
bitonality, 82, 113-116
Bonar, Horatius, 6
bourée, 44f, 47, 75f
Bull, Amos, 127
Byles, Mather and Samuel, 2

cadential broadening, 16, 25-28, 30, 41, 111, 132
Calvin's Psalter, 68
The Campbells are Coming, 47
Carpenter, —, 102f, 112
"cathedral" composers, 69, 124
Causton, Thomas, 68f
Cennick, John, 2
chaconne, 110, 134
changing metrical signatures, 38-42, 48,

51, 61f, 131-133. Cf. wrong barring
choosing notes, xvi, 98, 119-126, 129
Chopin, Frédéric, 101
chords, 84-87, 92, 94f, 99
Chorus, 21, 23f, 30, 35, 48, 70, 73f, 127-129, 132
chromaticism, 86-88
Church, John, xiv, 112, 124
"church" composers, 69, 93
clashes. See Elizabethan clashes and unjustified dissonance
coda, 38f, 106, 132, 134. See also Halle-lujah section
"Columbia, the gem of the ocean," 43f
C. M. (Common Meter), 2, 6, 19-21, 38f, 44, 68, 116, 125f, 132
counterpoint, 66-84, 91-93, 95f. See also fuguing
Country Gardens, 83
courante, 29
cross rhythms. See polyrhythms

dactylic meter, 5-7, 47f, 57
dances, 23, 25, 44f, 47-49, 75f, 138
Daniel, Oliver, xv
Daniel, R. T., ix, x, xiii, 14, 29, 57, 62, 66f, 84, 91, 100, 112
descriptive music, 56-58, 61, 70, 100-102, 107f, 134
Dickinson, Clarence, xv, xvi, 67, 83, 114f
diminished seventh chord, 85-87
diminished triad, 85
Dinneen, William, x
Dorian mode, 100, 107, 113, 136
dotted notes, 21, 34, 43, 45f, 50f, 58f, 61f, 64f

Elson, Louis, xi, 76-78, 99
Ehret, Walter, 114f
Eliot, Charlotte, 6
Elizabethan clash, 70, 87-91, 115f. cf. unjustified dissonance

Farmer, John, 90f
"The farmer in the dell," 43
Fellowes, E. H., 89
Flemming, F. F., 6
floridity, 28, 50-65, 70-73, 83, 103, 116, 130, 132, 134, 138
folk melody, 5, 43-50, 65, 105, 135. See dances
form, 61f, 110, 129, 132-137. See Chorus
free rhythms, 14, 29f, 32-38, 40-42
French, Jacob, 86, 115f
Frost, Maurice, 68f, 100
fuguing, xi, 17, 21, 24, 30, 38, 40, 44, 55, 59-61, 64-67, 69-84, 88, 91, 95, 99, 105, 114, 116, 124f, 127f, 130-132, 137

gavotte, 45
Genevan Psalter, 3, 33
German Psalter, 68
The girl I left behind me, 47
God Save the Queen, 7
Grainger, Percy, xiii, 83
Gram, Hans, xv, 96f
Greensleeves motive, 46, 110
Gregorian chant, 30f

Hallelujah motive, 59-61
Hallelujah section, 5, 10, 40f, 45f, 133
Handel, G. F., 59, 65, 124, 138
harmony. See chords, modes and modal harmony
Herbert, Petrus, 6
high notes, 121
H. M. (Hallelujah Meter), 3f
Holden, Oliver, xiv, 54, 113, 125f, 138
Howard, J. T., xi, xii, 67, 112

iambic meter, 2-8, 21, 44, 50, 76
illiteracy, xii, xiii, 69, 93-95
instruments, xv, xvi, 18f, 33, 52f, 67, 121f, 129
"Integer vitae," 6
Ionian mode, 100
Irish Washerwoman, 48

Jackson, G. P., ix
Jewish cantillation, 65, 138
jig, 5, 47f
Jocelyn, Simeon, 78, 125f
"Joy to the world," 73, 124

K-k-k-Katie, 128
Kethe, William, 68
keys, 60, 109, 118, 135f
Knapp, xiv, 38, 52, 54, 59, 67, 70, 86, 112, 124f

Landini cadence, 116-118
Lang, P. H., ix
Laus Deo (O. Holden), 127
Law, Andrew, xiv, 53f, 113, 124f
Lindstrom, C. E., xii, 67, 112
L. M. (Long Meter), 2, 18f, 33, 35f, 103, 113, 126, 129
"London Bridge is falling down," 43
Lowens, Irving, ix, x, xiii, 67, 76f, 79, 82-84, 91
ludicrous text repetition, 40, 73
Lully, J. B., 22, 65
Lydian mode, 100, 105
Lyon, James, xiv, 20, 54-56, 58, 86, 88, 113, 119f, 124, 126-130

Machaut cadence, 113-116, 118
Macdougal, H. C., xii, xiii, xiv, 14, 66f, 112, 133f, 136
Madan, Martin, 52f
madrigalism. See descriptive music
melismas, misplaced, 62-65
melody, 43-65. See also dances, floridity, folk melody.
Merbecke, John, 32
meter, poetic. See amphibrachic, anapestic, C.M., dactylic, H.M., lambic, L.M., P.M., Sapphic, S.M., spondaic, trochaic
meter, musical, 14-42. See changing metrical signatures
minuet, 22
Mixolydian mode, 91, 100, 113
modes and modal harmony, xvi, 79, 100-118, 136
modulation, lack of, 135
monotony, 100f, 121f, 133. See accidentals, lack of
Moravian anthems, xv
Morley, Thomas, 89
motet settings, 68f
musica ficta, 87, 111
Musikalischer Spass, 75
"My country, 'tis of thee," 7

neighboring notes, 84, 88, 90, 95
New Version (Tate and Brady), 1-5, 9-11, 56
New World Symphony, 44
ninth chords, 85, 87
notation, xiv

Old Version (Sternhold and Hopkins), 1-5, 34, 56, 100
Ol' Man River, 44, 62
organum, 95, 112, 114
Ott, Hans, 8

pandiatonicism, 99
parallel fifths and octaves, 27, 60, 70f, 79, 94, 102-106, 109, 112, 114, 117f 123, 133
parallel thirds, sixths, and tenths, 38, 62, 96-99, 126f, 129f
passing notes, 84, 88, 90, 117
Peck, John, 2
pentatonic scale, 94f
Peter, J. F., xv
Phrygian mode, 100, 106
Picardy third, 136
P.M. (Particular Meter), 2f, 48f, 55
P. M. (poet), 2
polyrhythms, 18, 30, 55, 57, 82
Pope, Alexander, 9, 46, 134
psalter (hymn book), 3, 5, 33, 68f
Psalter (prayer book), 9f
punctuation, 37, 39-42, 133
Purcell, Henry, 22, 65, 69

quartal harmony, 94f
quodlibet, 10-12, 41

Read, Daniel, xiv, 26, 33f, 62, 76, 78, 91, 105, 112, 115, 125, 162
refrain, 44, 131f
Relly, James and John, 1, 4-8, 13, 48f, 130
responsive treatment, 24, 124-131, 137
Revere, Paul, xiii
Rheingold, 101
rhythm and meter, 14-42. See also cadential broadening, changing metrical signatures, dotted notes, Hallelujah motive, wrong barring
rondo, 62, 129, 132f, 137
Rousseau, J. J., 94

St. Anne, 106
Sapphic meter, 6
sarabande, 23, 25
scales. See chromaticism, modes, pentatonic scale
Schenker, Heinrich, 110
Scholes, P. A., 73
Schubert, Franz, 14
Schumann, Robert, 15
Scotch snap, 21, 34, 43, 61f. See dotted notes
Scottish Psalter, 68f
sectionalized anthem, 131-137
Selby, William, 62, 97, 113
Senfl, Ludwig, 8
seventh chords, 27, 30, 84f, 87
shaped-note books, 93-95, 105

Shumway, Nehemiah, xiv, 21, 59f, 62, 79, 105, 113, 125
Slonimsky, Nicholas, 99
S.M. (Short Meter), 2, 20, 125
Smith, C. S., 67, 83
Southern Harmony (William Walker, 46, 92f.
Spaeth, Sigmund, 43
spondaic meter, 34
static harmony, 100f
Stephenson, Joseph, xv, 30, 76f, 79, 112
Sternhold and Hopkins. See Old Version
"Sumer is icumen in," 47
suspensions, lack of, 66
Swan, Timothy, 112f

Tans'ur, William, xiv, xv, 24-26, 30-33, 51, 57, 70, 75, 86, 99, 113, 119, 124, 129f
Tate, Nahum, 2
Tate and Brady. See New Version
texts, 1-13, 40, 62-65, 73, 128, 138
textual polyphony, 66f, 112
texture, 119-132, 137
tone painting. See descriptive music
tremolo, 57f
trills, 23, 135
trochaic meter, 5-7, 21, 34, 45
Tuckey, William, 62
Tudor composers, 56, 68f, 87, 90f
tunes in reports, 68f

unjustified dissonance, 70f, 91-93, 95f, 99. Cf. Elizabethan clashes

variation form, 110, 132, 134, 137
"Vom Himmel hoch," 109

Wassail Song, 47
"When I survey the wondrous cross," 120
Watts, Isaac, 1-6, 9, 11
Weelkes, Thomas, 87
Wesley, Charles, 1, 4-6, 78
West, Benjamin, 29f, 57, 84, 93
Westminster Carol, 44
Whitefield, George, 1
Williams, Aaron, xiv, 23, 25f, 33, 51, 58, 62, 70, 97, 113
Winkworth, Catherine, 6
Wise, Michael, 86
wrong barring, 14-37, 42, 50, 54f, 64, 70, 82, 91, 105, 136. Cf. Changing metrical signatures

Young, Edward, 9

DATE DUE

GAYLORD			PRINTED IN U.S.A